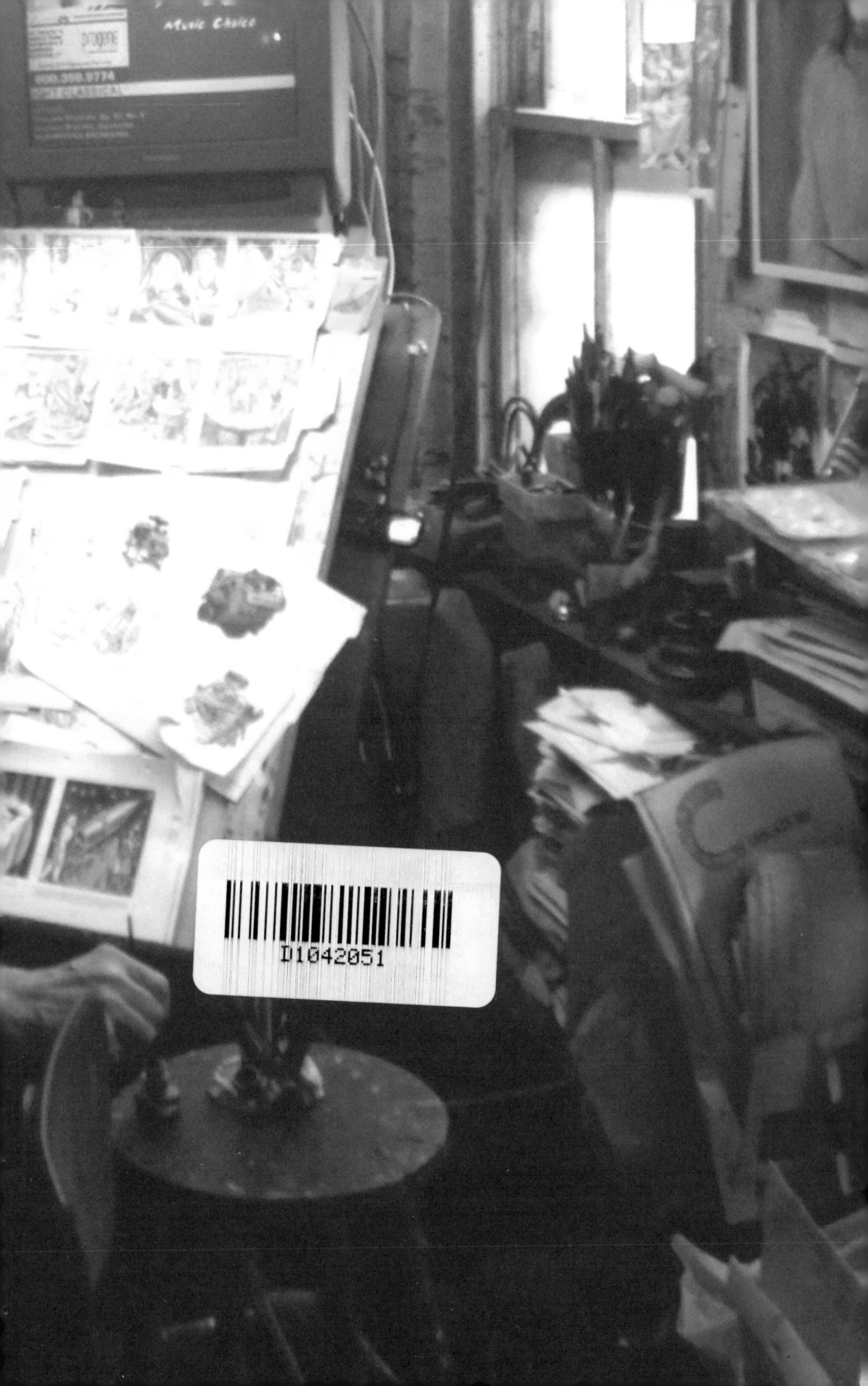
Music Choice
800.390.9774

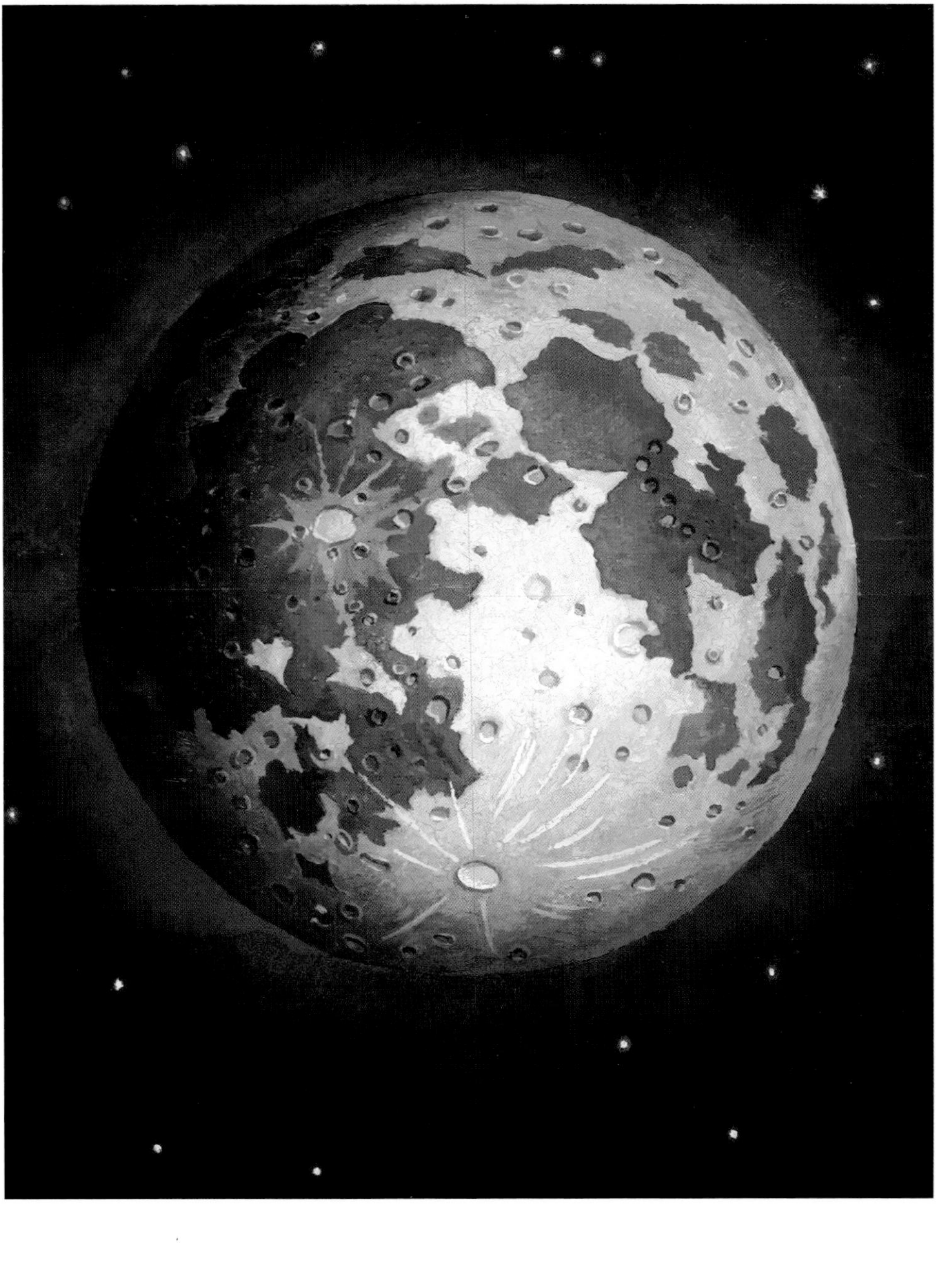

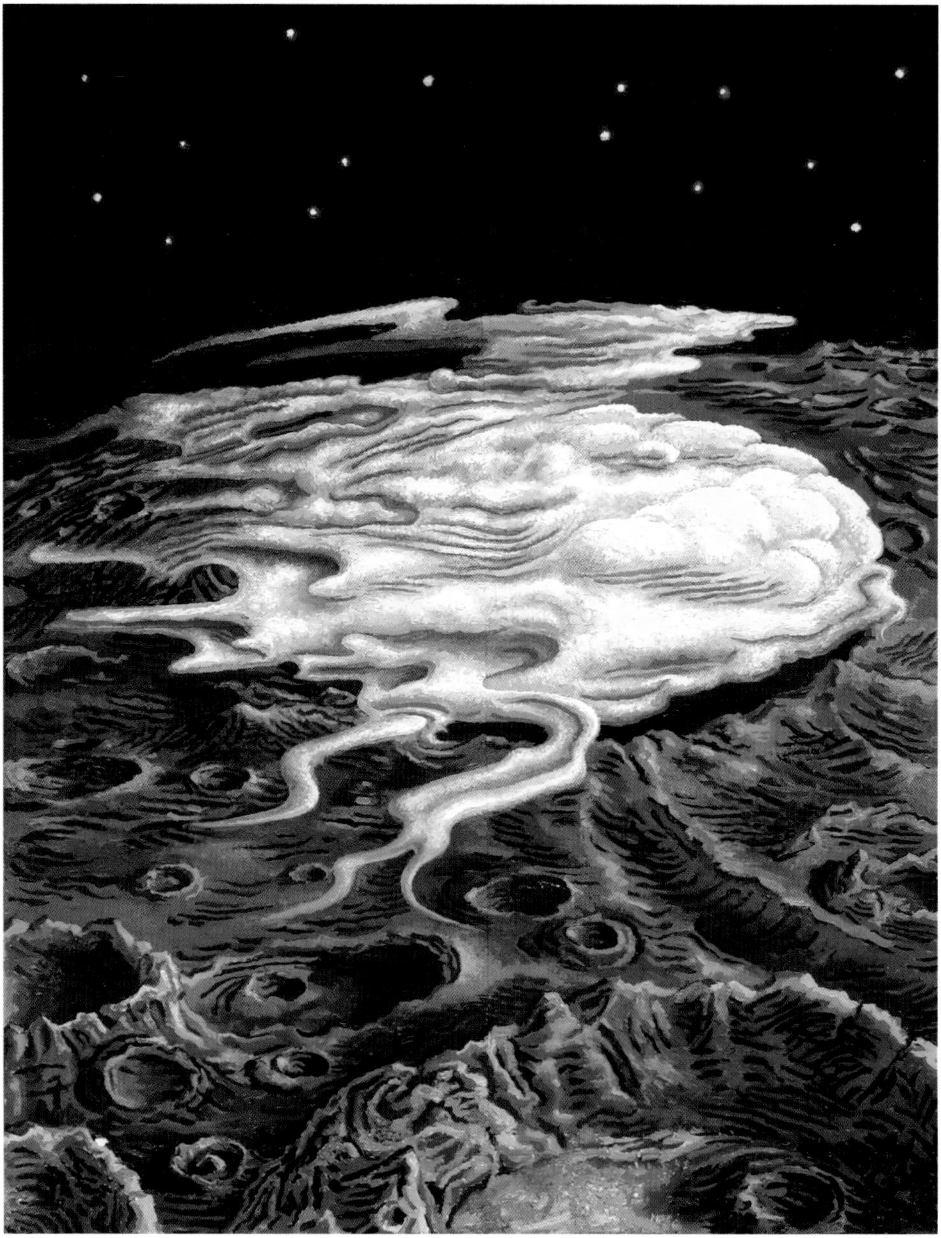

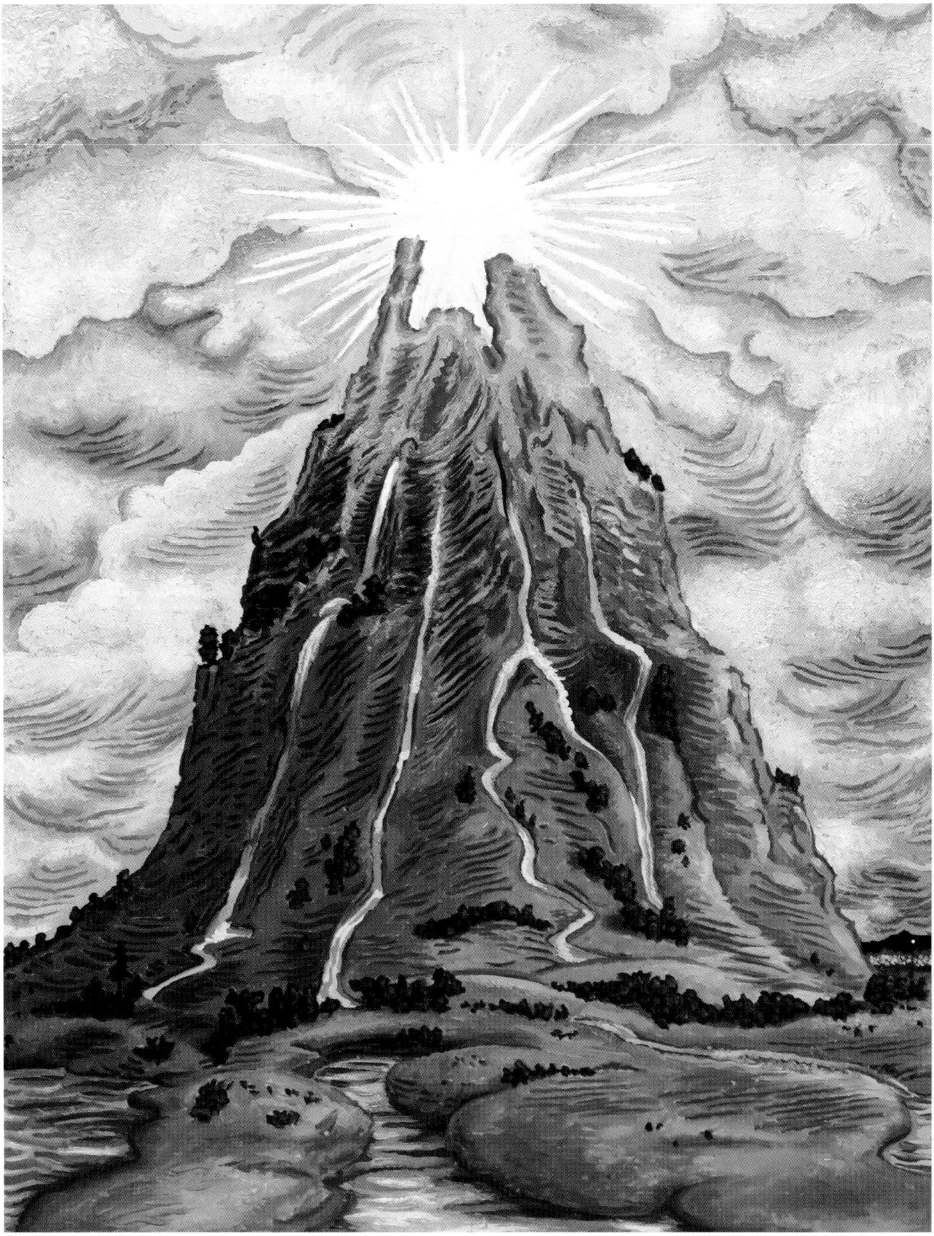

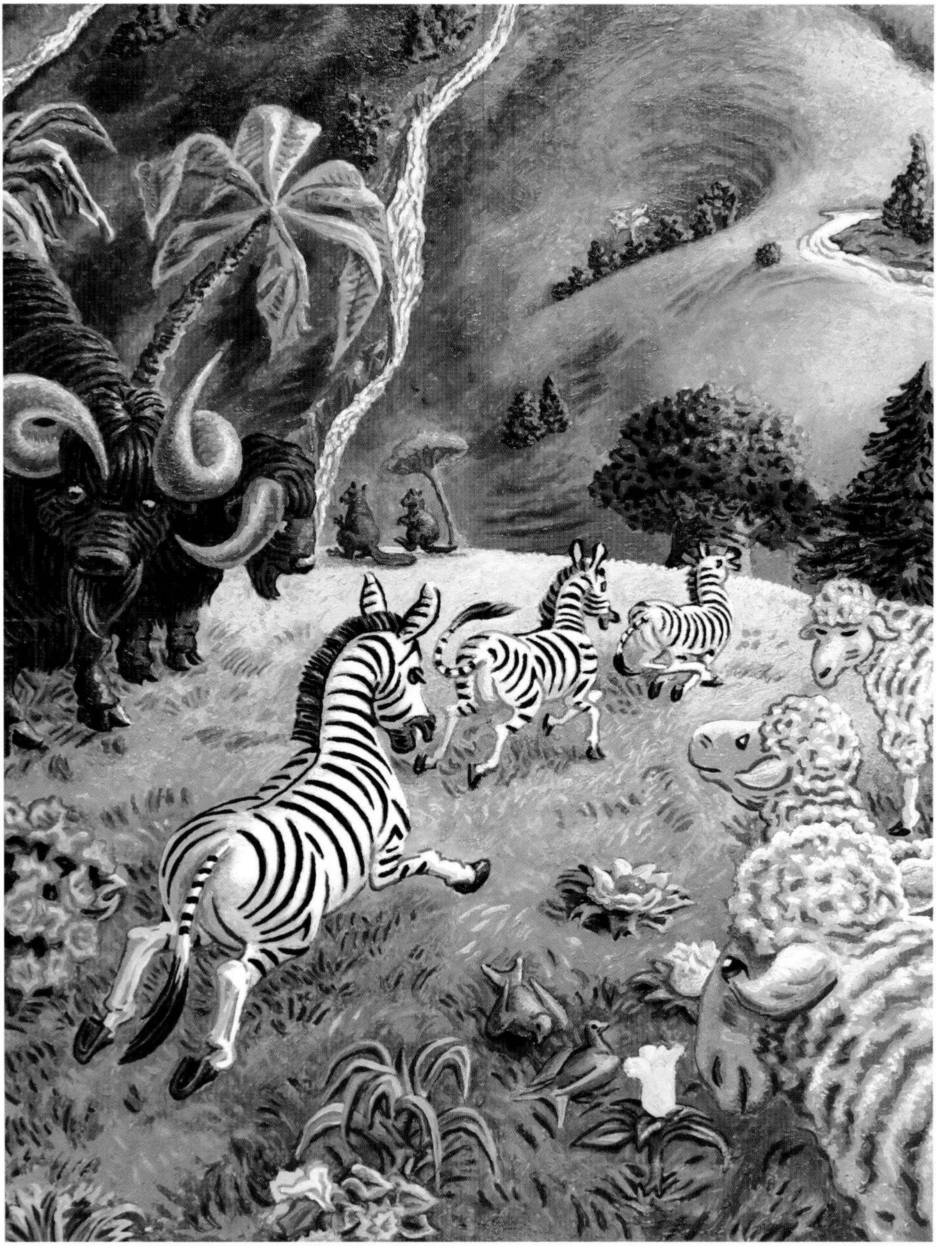

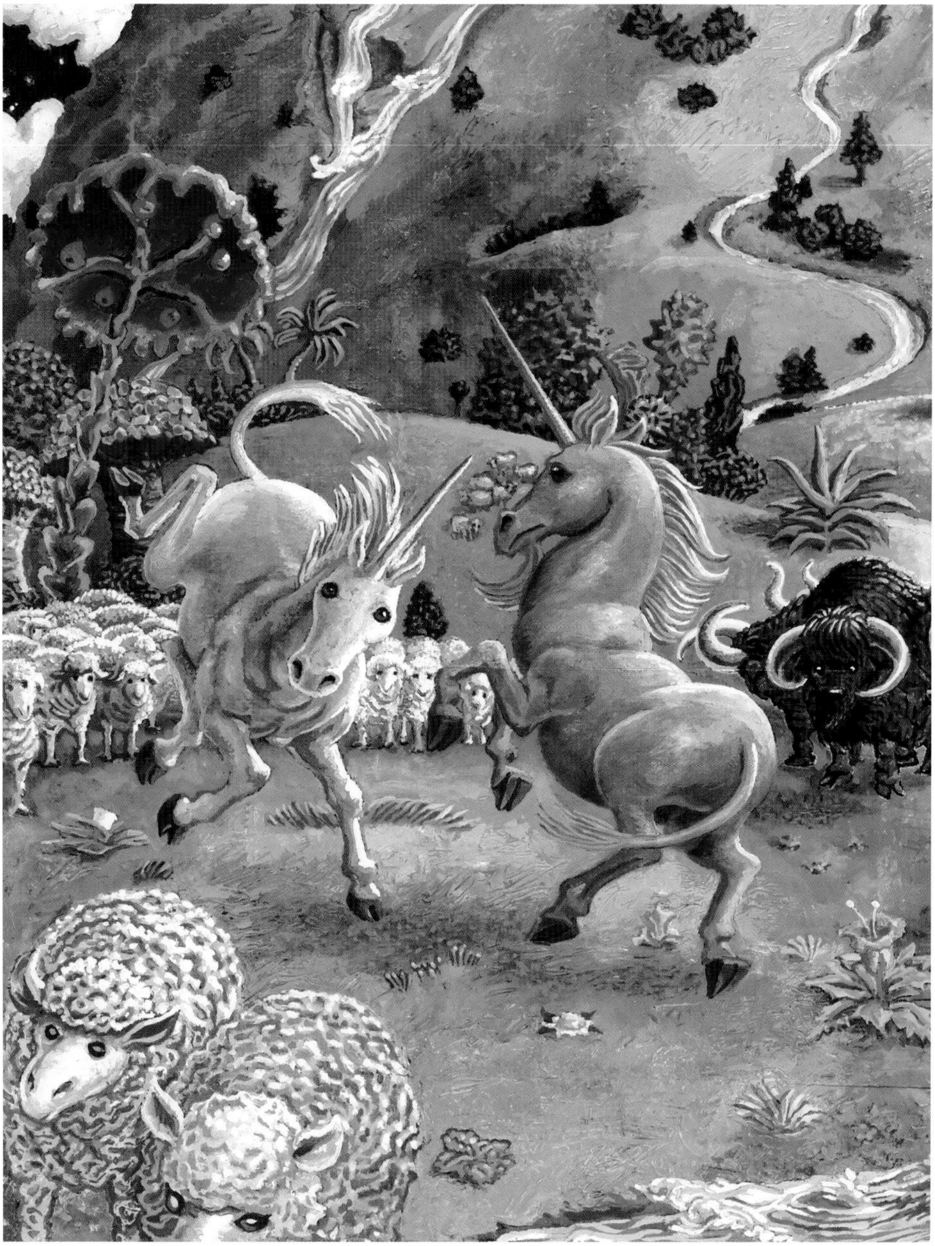

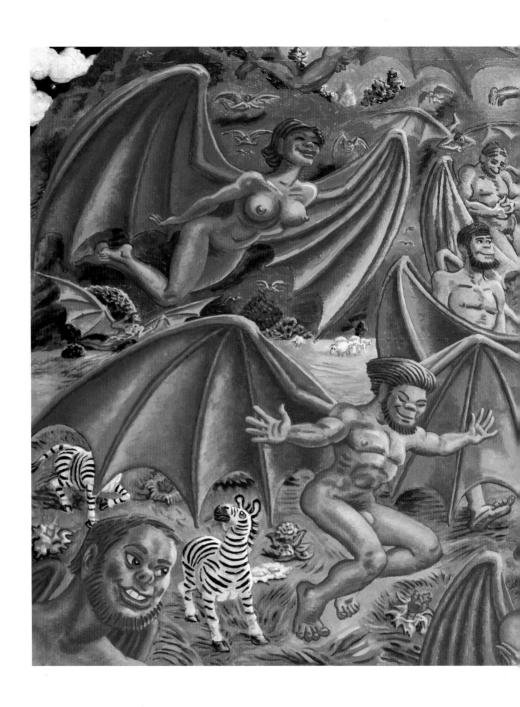

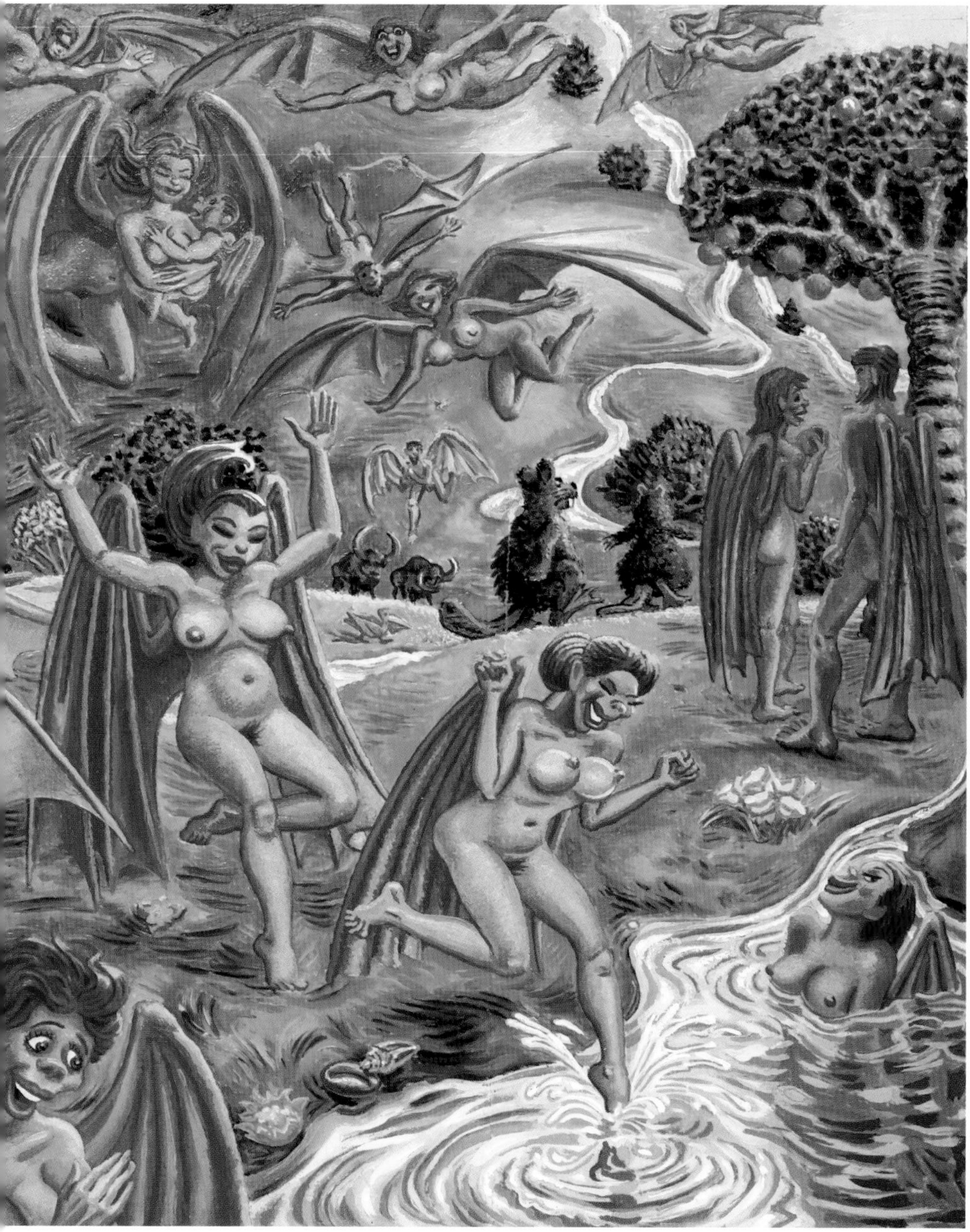

Life on the Moon is dedicated to
the memory of its author, Robert Grossman.

Creating this illustrated novel was a labor of love for him, and he considered it one of the greatest achievements of his storied career, if not his magnum opus. It represents a culmination of over fifty years spent drawing ingenious, hilarious, thought-provoking illustrations and comic strips, and combines so much of what interested him: history, fantasy, New York City, ideas, pictures, and words.

"When I was a kid," he once said, "I often thought books I read needed more pictures. One of the greatest capacities of pictures appeals to our abilities to formulate ideas, and we formulate our ideas with words. Most of what we consider to be great artworks of our culture throughout history relate to words. This picture-word thing is very intense." Indeed.

Robert Grossman found the process of originating his work "endlessly magical," and the idea that "there are an infinite number of little worlds" waiting to be put on paper excited him as much in his final years as it did when he was a child. With *Life on the Moon*, he has not only given us such a world, but he's one step ahead of us as always. Based on one of the earliest "fake news" stories ever documented, the book was entirely conceived prior to this era of "alternative facts." Sadly, Robert Grossman was taken from us too soon to see his illustrated novel in print, but he would be over the moon knowing that you're reading it right now.

We publish this book with heartfelt fondness and the highest respect for my departed friend, Robert.
Our deep thanks go the Grossman family and Richard Curtis.
—Craig Yoe

Cover design by Michael Grossman Rimbaud.
Dedication and endpapers photo of Robert Grossman working on *Life on the Moon* by Alex Emanuel Grossman.
Robert Grossman photo on page 398 by Leila Grossman.
Oil paintings by Robert Grossman, photographed by Annie Watt.
Executive Producer, Clizia Gussoni.

Robert Grossman's story reflects a period when some social mores were different than those of our more enlightened times. We trust the reader will understand.

YoeBooks.com: Craig Yoe & Clizia Gussoni, Chief Executive Officers and Creative Directors • Jeff Trexler, Attorney • Randall Cyrenne, Mark Lerer, Peter Sanderson, and Steven Thompson, Proofreaders • Steven Thompson, Publicist.

IDW Publishing: Chris Ryall, President, Publisher, & CCO • John Barber, Editor-In-Chief • Robbie Robbins, EVP/Sr. Art Director • Cara Morrison, Chief Financial Officer • Matt Ruzicka, Chief Accounting Officer • Anita Frazier, SVP of Sales and Marketing • David Hedgecock, Associate Publisher • Jerry Bennington, VP of New Product Development • Lorelei Bunjes, VP of Digital Services • Justin Eisinger, Editorial Director, Graphic Novels & Collections • Eric Moss, Senior Director, Licensing and Business Development
Ted Adams, IDW Founder

ISBN: 978-1-68405-456-5   22 21 20 19   1 2 3 4

LIFE ON THE MOON

ROBERT GROSSMAN

IDW PUBLISHING

IN 1781, the English astronomer William Herschel discovered the planet Uranus. He was aided by his sister Caroline, who also discovered eight new comets by herself. William Herschel believed that all the planets, as well as the Sun and the Moon, would one day be found to be inhabited.

In 1833, William's son, John Herschel, set sail for Cape Town, South Africa to study the skies of the Southern Hemisphere. He took with him the most powerful telescope ever built.

NEW YORK CITY, summer, 1835. The largest city in America, population 200,000, is well known for the energy and brash enterprise of its citizens. Richard Adams Locke, the young editor of *The New York Sun*, takes an afternoon walk heading west down Canal Street.

The Sun is only two years old. It is the first newspaper ever to sell for a mere penny. One of its innovations is the hiring of poor children to hawk the daily edition in the streets. These urchins have come to be known as "newsboys."

Feral swine roam the streets of New York, tolerated for their garbage-eating capability. Descended from domesticated animals, some of them, over time, have reverted to a pre-domestication razorback form.

A certain sow being driven to market has suddenly attracted the attention of a large wild boar.

Richard Locke sees an accident about to happen. He vaults over the herd,

and sweeps a young woman out of the path of the charging beast.

"You brute!" the woman shouts, and strikes Locke with her parasol.

She runs to a passing cab and in a moment is gone.

"I saw what you done, Mr. Locke," says Joey the newsboy, "Ladies is dangerous."

"You may be right, Joey," says Locke.

Locke is a descendant of the philosopher John Locke (1632-1704), who taught that the mind is a blank slate upon which experience leaves its mark—in this case, a growing bump on the man's forehead.

Locke turns right on Broadway and heads uptown.

Back on Canal Street, a man hands Joey a package and a small coin. "See your guv'nor gets this, laddie," he says.

Locke makes his way to Niblo's Garden at the northeast corner of Prince Street and Broadway.

Niblo's advertises "The Greatest Curiosity In The World." Locke's newspaper has reported the story, but Locke wants to see Joice Heth for himself.

In Niblo's grand salon, a framed bill of sale documents the purchase by Augustine Washington of Joice Heth, a slave born in Madagascar.

Augustine was the father of George Washington. Joice Heth was the infant George Washington's nurse. She is 161 years old.

Joice Heth is blind and bedridden and evidently has no use for manicures or dentistry. But she speaks clearly of her time on the Washington plantation, and fondly of her "dear little Georgie."

When he was a baby, the future president pissed in her eye. When he chopped down the cherry tree, she made a cobbler. His favorite nursery rhyme was *Twinkle Twinkle Little Star*, and she sings the whole thing.

Locke talks with the proprietor of the exhibition, a young man from Connecticut named Barnum.

"I was a grocer until this year," says Barnum. "I bought Joice for $500 and it's strictly the curiosity business for me from now on. When I think of all the time I wasted weighing carrots, cheese, and cabbages it makes me sick."

"In a grocery, spoilage can kill you, but I figure old Joice still has a few good years left in her. I feed her mostly gin and she's making me a bundle. By the way, for an additional 25 cents I can take you backstage where she'll show you the very first tits that the father of our country ever sucked."

"And for another two bits, she'll let you suck 'em," Barnum adds.

"I've had enough excitement for today," says Locke.

"That's a pretty nice bump on your forehead," says Barnum.

"A woman hit me with her parasol," says Locke.

"You dog," says Barnum.

"But if you can get it to grow some more you could become a valuable curiosity: The Unicorn Man."

Locke leaves Niblo's pondering this new potential career path.

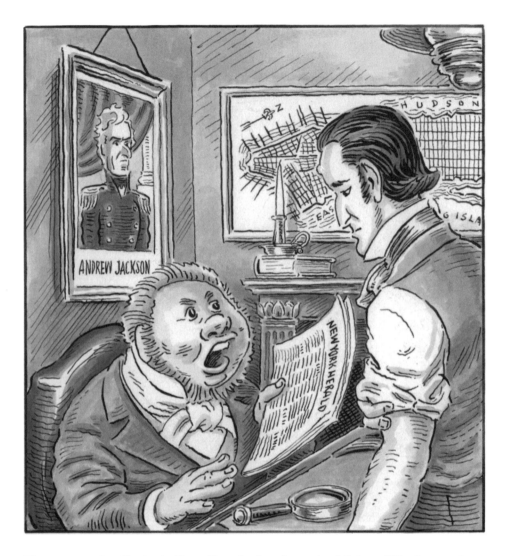

The next morning, Benjamin Henry Day, the founder and publisher of *The Sun*, goads Locke. *The Sun* is losing readers to James Gordon Bennett's upstart daily, the *Herald*. Something must be done.

"And by the way," he says, "what happened to your head?"

In his own office, Locke is sharpening a pen when Joey hands him a package. "A man give me this for you," he says.

"Thank you, Joey," says Locke. On his way out Joey says, "There's a lady waiting in the hall to see you, sir."

"You!" they say simultaneously.

"Please don't hit me again," says Locke.

"So you are the editor," says the lady, "I owe you an apology. The cabman said you saved me from a rampaging beast."

"But there is another beast rampaging in our country and its name is slavery. It has been against the law in New York for eight years, but it must be abolished everywhere. And now there is a man here named Barnum who boasts of owning Joice Heth."

The young woman's name is Charity Moore. She has written an indignant letter to the editor. After condemning slavery, she asks, "Is there not philanthropy enough in America to take care of one who is the sole remaining tie to the man who was 'first in war, first in peace, and first in the hearts of his countrymen'?"

Her letter concludes, "We should protect and honor Joice Heth and not suffer her to be put on show, like a trained animal, to fill the coffers of mercenary men."

Locke takes the letter from her, and promises it will be printed.

"Oh, your poor head," Charity says.

"I'm so sorry I hurt you," says Charity. "You should put ice on it."

"I did," says Locke.

"Sit down," says Charity.

"Let me have a look," she says, and gently touches Locke's forehead.
Locke feels his heart do a little gavotte.

"My God, it's gone," says Locke, "How did you do that?"

"I have unusually cold hands," says Charity Moore.

They go to the composing room, where Locke tells Fortune, the typesetter, to prepare Miss Moore's letter for the next edition.

Locke sees the woman out of the building and into a cab on William Street.

Back in his office, Locke opens the package the boy left for him.

The package contains a copy of the latest issue of the *Edinburgh Journal of Science*. In it is the most astonishing news Locke has ever read.

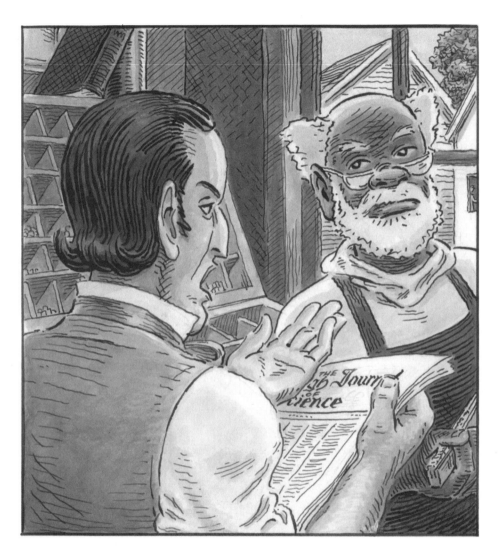

Locke brings the *Journal* to Fortune and instructs him to set its entire contents in type. It's a rush job. The *Sun* is going to be first to publish the story in America.

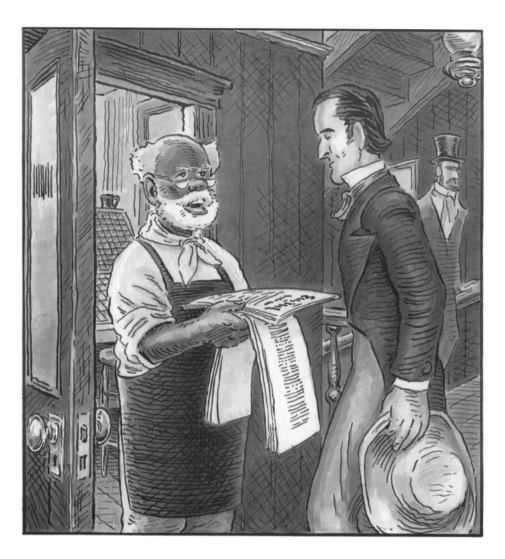

The next morning, the galley proofs are ready.

"That's some story, Mr. Locke," says Fortune. It is the first time the editor has ever heard the typesetter comment on a story he has set.

Locke brings the galleys to the publisher.

"This is going to get us some readers, Ben," says Locke.

Day begins to read.

"Good stuff," Day finally says, "but something's missing: it needs art—pictures."
He gives Locke the name of an artist he knows of who will work fast and cheap.

The artist lives in Harlem. Locke walks to the wharf on Desbrosses Street. A steamboat, the mechanical marvel of the age, will take him uptown.

As the boat passes West 3rd Street, the city gives way to farms and open countryside. A grid system for developing the whole island of Manhattan has existed since 1811, but so far its implementation is largely theoretical.

Locke finds the artist's house.

A woman comes to the door. She urges Locke to be quiet. "My husband is hunting," she says.

They tiptoe through the house to the kitchen, where the artist poises motionless at the windowsill.

With one majestic swoop, he captures and strangles two birds.

"Fine specimens of *columba livia*—in other words: lunch!" he shouts, and then, "Lucy, who is this man?"

Locke introduces himself. Mr. Audubon invites him to dine with them, catches another pigeon and deftly skins and eviscerates the birds, remarking, "Never eat the skin. It will only make you fat."

"Food always comes first—Jean Jacques is French, you know," Lucy tells Locke. "In fact," she adds in a low voice, "he is the long lost dauphin, the son of Louis XVI, but you must never bring it up."

They eat in the garden. With freshly picked *haricots verts* and Lucy's homemade beer, it is a fine meal.

Afterward, Locke gives the artist the *Edinburgh Journal of Science* and explains that *The Sun* is reprinting it. There are certain natural phenomena described in the article that require illustration, he tells him.

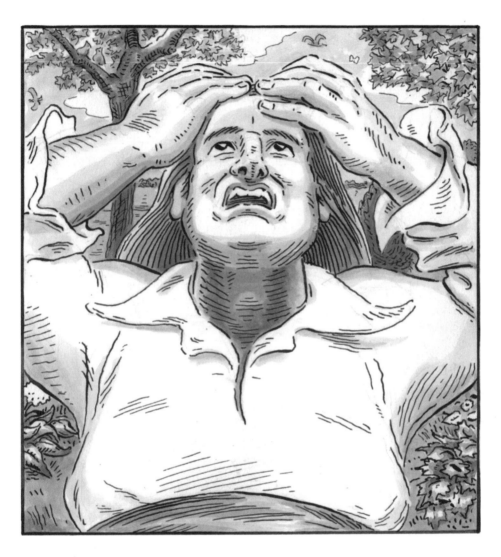

"To think," says Audubon, "that the rightful heir to the Bourbon throne at Versailles should be reduced to doing illustrations for a vulgar gazette. *Mon Dieu!*"

He accepts the job and promises the finished work in two days.

Two days later, Audubon brings the artwork to *The Sun*. Day and Locke pronounce the work satisfactory. Day notices that none of the drawings are signed.

"I never sign a picture of anything I haven't personally killed," says Audubon. He is paid and leaves.

"Now let's get this story on the street," says Day.

On the morning of Tuesday, August 25, 1835, the first installment of the story is published and sells briskly. It is headlined,

GREAT ASTRONOMICAL DISCOVERIES
LATELY MADE
BY SIR JOHN HERSCHEL, L.L.D F.R.S. &c

At the Cape of Good Hope
[From the *Edinburgh Journal of Science*]

It tells in scientific detail how Sir John Herschel designed and built a powerful new telescope and brought it to the Cape of Good Hope to make discoveries, "which will confer upon the present generation of the human race a proud distinction through all future time."

Herschel's great telescope, *The Sun* reports, has enabled him to see astronomical objects in unprecedented detail. The story will continue on the following day.

In the second installment, *The Sun* tells how on the night of January 10, 1835, while studying the pitted and mountainous surface of the Moon, Herschel observed vaporous matter emanating from a region near the northwestern limb of the sphere, close to the *Mare Imbrium*.

Applying increasing powers of magnification, Herschel was able to move in closer, so to speak, to the area of this mysterious emanation which resembled nothing so much as earthly clouds.

Adjusting his instrument to peer beneath the clouds, Herschel realized he was looking into a vast basin whose inner escarpment glittered with huge crystals. A mountaintop in the foreground appeared to be covered with a field of *Papaver Rhoeas*—poppies, "the first organic production of nature in a foreign world ever revealed to the eyes of men."

66

The next morning, Day congratulates Locke. The Herschel story is attracting readers. Yesterday's edition sold 7,500 copies instead of the usual 5,000. Pressmen are working around the clock.

Day gives Locke a cigar.

To keep pace with demand, *The Sun* has hired additional newsboys and even some newsgirls as the third installment of "Great Astronomical Discoveries" goes on sale.

The Herschel story resumes, as the astronomer's view continues down the crystalline cliffs that have been discovered. Near the bottom, "We were at length delighted to perceive that novelty, a lunar forest."

Some of the lunar trees resembled yews and firs like those on Earth, while others were entirely unfamiliar.

Suddenly, atop one exotic plant, a magnificent golden-eyed bird alit, "blessing our panting hopes for a specimen of conscious existence," says Herschel.

He was now able to see that the lunar forest ended abruptly at the shore of a quiet lake or inland sea.

In the center of Herschel's view, an island or headland appeared to be the source of the vapors that filled the great basin.

On Friday morning, Locke watches the unloading of *The Sun*'s first steam-powered printing press. Ben Day had determined it was the only way to keep up with the public's appetite for more "Great Astronomical Discoveries."

Friday's edition of *The Sun* recounts how Herschel focused in on what was now clearly a volcanic peak, incandescent at the top, with cataracts and streams descending to the lunar sea. At one point, a great fish surfaced in the astronomer's field of vision, followed by many smaller ones.

Saturday's *Sun*, the first to be printed by steam power, has a press run of 15,000 and sells out immediately.

At the foot of the volcanic mountain, Herschel has discovered a broad green "champaign district."

And there, among the low hills, woods, and meadows, he finds an abundance of lunar animals—herds of small bison with peculiar horns, sheep "which would not have disgraced the farms of Leicestershire," large beavers who walked upright and carried their young in their arms, and pelicans indistinguishable from the earthly variety.

And then Herschel reports, "springing from the green turf with all the unaccountable antics of young lambs or kittens," a pair of unicorns. At this point, *The Sun* once again prints, "To be continued."

Newspapers don't appear in New York on the Sabbath, but this Sunday the ministers in Grace Church, Trinity Church and perhaps others cite *The Sun*'s revelations as new evidence of the existence of a bounteous Creator, compare the rich lunar landscape to that of the pristine American West, and hail Sir John Herschel as a latter-day Christopher Columbus.

Early Monday morning, Benjamin Day is gratified to see a large crowd gathering in front of *The Sun*'s building, eager for the newest installment of "Great Astronomical Discoveries."

When the paper appears, readers are not disappointed. Herschel continues to observe animal life on the Moon. Remarkably, his telescope has brought into focus a group of miniature zebras.

Herschel then reports, " We were thrilled with astonishment to perceive a flock of large winged creatures, unlike any kind of birds, descend from the hills with a slow, even motion and alight by a stream."

To his colleagues he says, "Now here we have something worth looking at."

The creatures looked much like human beings—red-haired with a "faintly simian aspect" about the face. But they each had a pair of membranous wings that they kept folded when not flying.

Herschel gave them the scientific name *Vespertilio-homo,* or man-bat.

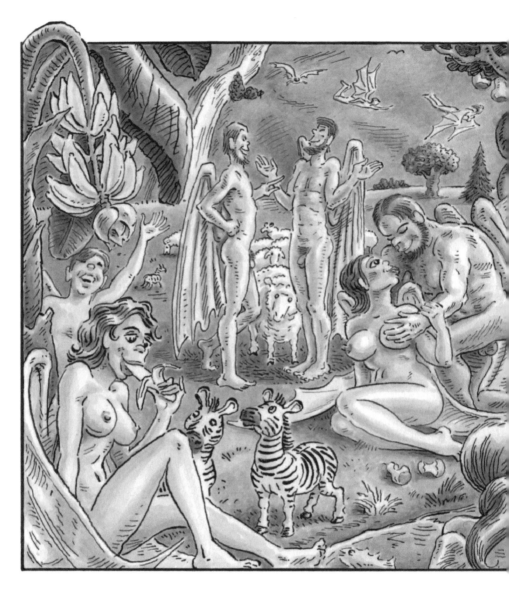

Studying the telescopic image of the man-bats, who were of both sexes, Herschel observed, "they were evidently engaged in conversation; their gesticulation appeared impassioned and emphatic. We hence inferred that they were rational beings. They are doubtless innocent and happy creatures, notwithstanding that some of their amusements would but ill comport with our terrestrial notions of decorum."

As dawn comes on January 11th and the Moon sinks out of view, Herschel thinks of Byron's words in *Childe Harold's Pilgrimage:*

Meek Diana's crest,
Floats through the azure air, an island of the blest.

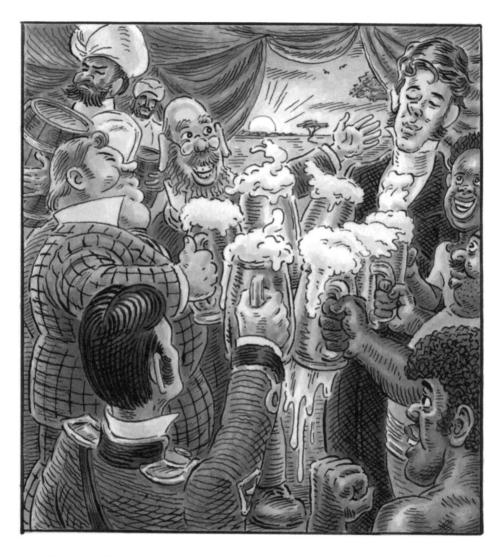

Immediately, Dr. Herschel gathers his associates, Dr. Andrew Grant, Lieutenant Drummond of the Royal Engineers, Herbert Home Esq., and all their assistants "to reward their vigilant attention with congratulatory bumpers of the best 'East Indian Particular.'"

Grant raises a toast "to Sir John Herschel, who has built an imperishable monument to the age in which we live."

That day at noon, inadvertently, perhaps as a consequence of the early morning ale, the Sun was permitted to shine directly into the unattended telescope, the concentrated rays instantly setting it on fire.

Until the great instrument is repaired, Herschel regrets he will have nothing further to report. And so *The Sun*'s series, "Great Astronomical Discoveries," comes to an end.

Benjamin Day is jubilant. Yesterday's edition of *The Sun* sold 19,000 copies. *The London Times* has never sold more than 17,000. *The New York Sun* is the largest-selling newspaper in the world. Day gives Locke two cigars.

Day receives a letter of grudging admiration from his competitor, James Gordon Bennett of the *Herald*:

Day, you bastard. How the hell did you get hold of that Moon story before we did? I feel like you've gouged out my balls with a razor sharp scoop. Fuck you.

Your Obedient Servant, etc.

Hmm, we scooped them, Day thinks, a nice turn of phrase.

Locke, too, gets a letter. It is from Charity Moore:

Dear Mr. Locke,

The power of the printed word in these modern times cannot be underestimated. No sooner had my letter denouncing the slaver, Barnum, appeared in The Sun, *than the beast fled New York City.*

Barnum was leaving anyway, Locke thinks, he had engagements in Philadelphia and Baltimore.

The letter continues:

> The Sun*'s recent series on Dr. Herschel's discoveries has been of great interest to my father, the Reverend Clement Moore. He would like to meet you.*

She asks Locke to come to tea on Thursday. Her letter has a faint aroma of honey and soap.

Clement Moore is not only a leading theologian, he is also one of the city's richest men. The Moore family estate, Chelsea, is splendid.

A butler admits Locke. Charity greets him. He has brought her a nosegay and, although Locke sees his flowers are entirely superfluous, Charity gushes over them.

"Forget-me-nots! Really, Mr. Locke."

She introduces Locke to her father.

"Sir," says Moore, "I am in your debt. My daughter tells me you saved her from being trampled by a savage animal."

Then he congratulates Locke on *The Sun*'s recent success. He has learned that Locke's newspaper is now printed by steam power.

Moore has important investments in the mining and distribution of coal. He gives Locke the name of a merchant who will sell coal to *The Sun* at an "advantageous price." "The man might even be persuaded to purchase a small advertisement," he adds.

Locke thanks the reverend and tells him to consider his debt repaid.

They sit down. Moore introduces the elderly gentleman as Signor Da Ponte, a professor of Italian at Columbia College.

"Well, Mr. Locke," says Moore, "it is a marvelous time we are living in when the hidden works of the Creator are revealed to mankind in a lowly one-a-penny handbill."

"It is, sir," says Locke diplomatically.

Tea is served. Charity, her father, and Da Ponte clink teacups and say, "L'chaim." Locke looks confused.

'This is an abstinent household," says Da Ponte, "so they toast with tea. Clement is the author of *The Compendious Lexicon of the Hebrew Language*, and I was born a Jew in Venice. *L'chaim* means 'to life' in Hebrew."

Locke raises his cup and says, "L'chaim."

"Dr. Herschel's discovery of life on the Moon raises a number of philosophical questions, does it not Mr. Locke?" says Moore.

"How so?" says Locke.

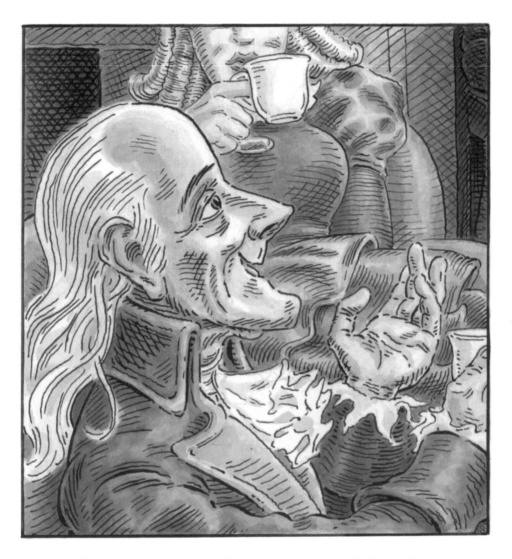

"I knew William Herschel, the present Herschel's father," says Da Ponte. "I met him when I was in England with Wolfie."

"Signor Da Ponte is referring to Herr Mozart the composer," says Moore, "Lorenzo wrote *libretti* for his operas."

"Only the good ones," says Da Ponte.

"William Herschel was born in Germany," says Da Ponte. "His father was a Jew. They were all musicians. Herschel's sister Caroline had the voice of an angel. William played the oboe and was a fine composer. I wrote lyrics for one of his tunes. If you'd like, I could sing them."

"Charity," says Moore, "Why don't you take Lorenzo into the library and help him rehearse his song. Perhaps you can accompany him on your Wheatstone. There are some matters I'd like to discuss with Mr. Locke."

They leave to rehearse. "Such an amusing man," says Moore. "And now, as I was saying: the questions raised by Herschel's discoveries. First of all, were the creatures on the Moon created on the fourth day, when God created the Moon, or on the sixth day, when He created animals and man on Earth?"

"For it seems that the *Vespertilio-homo* is a kindred species to our own and, according to the astronomer, capable of rational thought. Since they are unclothed, we must wonder whether, perhaps, they are living in an innocent, unfallen state—Herschel detected no serpents on the Moon."

"Maybe none of the fruit on the Moon was forbidden," Locke offers.

"Then again," says Moore, "it is possible that our Savior has appeared on the Moon and had more success there than here in establishing a perpetual paradisical condition."

"It would be wonderful to be able to communicate with the *Vespertilio*, but of course we would need to know what language they speak. I believe there can be only one answer to that question: the oldest, purest tongue we know, that of the Lord Himself—Hebrew uncontaminated by later Aramaic and Greek inclusions."

Moore imagines a system whereby the open space of the American West would be turned into a vast signboard. Large quantities of a material of a contrasting color to that of the prairie—coal would be ideal—would be transported there, and arranged to spell out Hebrew words visible to the inhabitants of the Moon.

"Of course," says Moore, "the Sahara desert, being larger and more centrally located on the globe, would be a more highly visible location, but shipping all the coal there would probably be impractical."

Moore continues. "Once communication has been established and the Moon folk know we can see them with a telescope, they can signal back to us using semaphore flags."

Moore tells Locke he is preparing a sermon in which he will expound on these ideas at greater length. Would Locke be good enough to send a reporter to cover the sermon for *The Sun*? Locke assures him he will.

Charity and Da Ponte return from the library ready to perform William Herschel's music, with lyrics by Da Ponte. Charity brings her Wheatstone "concertina," a new musical invention and the first one Locke has seen.

Da Ponte introduces the song. Herschel senior was known to his friends as "Heshie."
Da Ponte is sorry to tell Moore that Heshie detested religion. He lost his position as a
kapellmeister after failing to hide his contempt for the liturgy. The lasting obloquy of
the clerics led him to take up astronomy as a new career.

The song has many verses and a delightful refrain:

So here's to Heshie Herschel,
'Cause his telescopic search'll,
Bring him fame, instead of shame,
The way he winced in church'll.

"I'd no idea that Herschel had been all that controversial," says Moore, and then, "Ha! I am a poet!"

"Not many people know that Clement wrote *The Night Before Christmas*," Da Ponte tells Locke. Locke knows the poem.

"Pardon my blushes," says Moore.

Out of curiosity, Locke lifts the concertina and it makes an impolite noise. He realizes it is time to leave. Da Ponte invites Locke to dinner at his home a few days hence.

"Be careful," says Moore, "the Italians hold the strange belief that the tomato is not a deadly poison."

Charity sees Locke to his waiting cab. They agree to meet Monday afternoon for a promenade in the Castle Garden.

At the southern tip of Manhattan, the Castle Garden had once been a fort but now is the chief gathering place for recreation and amusement in the city. And today New York is a city that has gone Moon-mad.

A Chinese woman is selling "Moon cakes." Another woman hawks a chocolate confection she calls a "Moon pie."

A sailor is displaying a pet bat. *The Sun*'s newsboys sell a pamphlet version of "Great Astronomical Discoveries." Locke and Charity meet.

"I see you left the parasol at home," says Locke.

"Yes, I am unarmed," says Charity.

"Father liked you," says Charity. "He thinks your role as a kind of celestial messenger has elevated you above the rank of tradesman, and he is now willing to consider that something printed in a 'one-a-penny handbill' may have nearly the significance of Holy Writ."

"That looks like Stilton," says Locke.

Locke learns more about Charity. She is the youngest of the Moore children. Their mother is dead. Her older brother, Benjamin, disappointed their father by not entering the clergy, went to Paris to study art under Ingres, and now manufactures house paint in Brooklyn.

Charity was tutored at home, is well educated, and freely occupies herself tending to the blind, the deaf, the ill, the poor, the bereaved, and sometimes just shopping. She is dedicated to the goal of the new American Anti-Slavery Society—immediate emancipation of all slaves—but admits that, with Congress deadlocked on the issue, she has no idea how emancipation will ever be achieved.

'Tell me about yourself, Mr. Locke," says Charity. He was born in England, Locke relates, educated at Cambridge, his parents are dead. He considered emulating Byron and fighting the Turks in Greece, thought better of it, came to America lured by curiosity and stayed, captivated by its "sense of endless possibility"—quite distinct from the settled nature of the Old World.

A man has calculated that on the Moon, since it is smaller than the Earth, things would weigh less. He has changed the dial on his scale accordingly. Locke asks Charity if she'd like to try it.

"Oh, I'm so fat," says Charity.

On the Moon, Charity would weigh 19 pounds. Locke tells her that the Bowery Theatre will soon be presenting a show based on *The Sun*'s recent series. Would Miss Moore, all 19 pounds of her, care to join him for the opening night performance? Miss Moore says she would be honored.

The first installment of *The Sun*'s story on Herschel's discoveries appeared on a day when the Moon was new and barely visible. Now, fourteen days later, while the Sun has not quite set, the people in Castle Garden stare transfixed as a full, yellow Harvest Moon rises over the harbor.

A man has set up a telescope and charges people a penny to look through it. Locke puts his eye to the instrument and sees an even larger full, yellow Harvest Moon, although no unicorns, zebras or bat people are in evidence. Charity looks through the telescope and says in a low voice, "It's glorious."

In her parlor at Chelsea, Charity has her hair done for the coming Bowery Theatre premiere. Her hairdresser is Pierre, a favorite of the well-to-do women of New York. With Charity is her friend Julia Ward, who will also attend the opening.

Pierre is a former slave from Haiti. A devout man, he goes to morning Mass daily at St. Peter's on Barclay Street.

"Do you think, Pierre, that heaven—the place we go when we die—could possibly be on the Moon?" she asks.

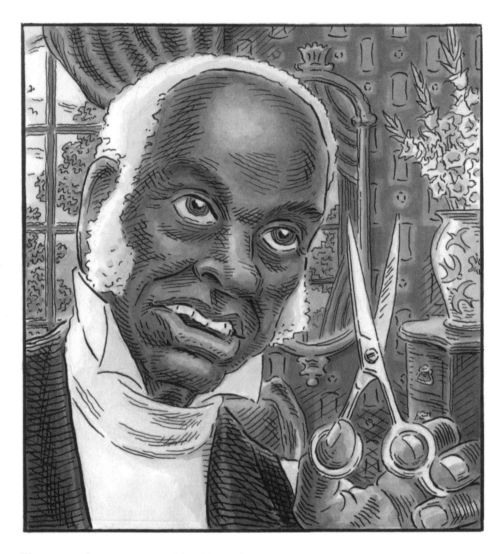

"I'm not much on astronomy, Miss Moore," says Pierre, "but I know that for many of my people, hell is right here on earth."

Like Charity and Julia, Pierre is a member of the Anti-Slavery Society, but he fears emancipation will not come soon, and not without powerful leadership and much shedding of blood.

He speaks of the great liberator Toussaint L'Ouverture who led the slave rebellion in Haiti, ruled the island justly, successfully fought the French, the British and Spanish, yet died a martyr's death in Napoleon's prison.

To remind himself of the struggles of the past and those that lie ahead, Pierre carries on his watch chain a relic of L'Ouverture: one of his molars mounted in silver.

"His tooth is marching on," says Julia.

The hairdresser's work is outstanding. When Locke calls on Charity to take her to the theatre she greets him with her hair done in Pierre's interpretation of lunar bat wings.

Julia's auburn tresses have been fashioned by Pierre into a silken simulacrum of Herschel's famous telescope. Accompanying Julia tonight will be Mr. Howe, a visitor from Boston.

Like Charity, Sam Howe is a teacher of the blind. In the carriage, the two talk about the method of reading by touch recently developed by Monsieur Braille.

Howe, too, is a member of the Anti-Slavery Society, but he disapproves of Julia's and Charity's participation in politics.

"Before we know it, the ladies will be demanding the right to vote," he jokes, but no one laughs.

The Bowery is New York's leading theater. Locke, Charity, Julia and Mr. Howe arrive for the premiere performance of *Moonbeams, or Lunar Discoveries*.

A minstrel band sets the scene in Africa as they croon a nostalgic Negro melody, *Midnight Upon The Old Zambezi*. The curtains part and we meet a handsome young astronomer named Johnny.

As he swivels his scientific instrument, Johnny sings,

I built a great all-seeing eye,
New knowledge to discover,
But fear that neither earth nor sky,
Will tender me a lover.

A chemical green limelight, the latest development in theatre technology, suddenly reveals a fabulous creature.

Tonight must be my lucky day, Johnny sings,
Behold upon the Moon,
A girl who takes my breath away,
I'll call her Claire de Lune.

As Claire sings while flittering above the stage, we learn that she too is lonely. Johnny reaches out to her, but alas, it seems the most hopeless of loves because they live in two different worlds.

Before the second act, the house manager takes the stage, saying, "We are happy to have in the audience tonight the man who gave to the New World the wonderful news of life on another world: Mr. Richard Locke of *The New York Sun*."

As Act II begins, we are on the Moon. Mr. Castorman, a real estate developer, holds a mortgage on the tree which is Claire's home. He'll forgive the loan if Claire will marry him. Otherwise, he will chop down her tree with his teeth.

Castorman speaks with a German accent reminiscent of that of John Jacob Astor, America's richest man and a New Yorker. Happily, Astor is not in tonight's audience, as Castorman describes a scheme to subdivide the Moon into rectangular plots and erect multi-story beaver lodges on every one of them.

Claire is distraught. She tells her sad tale to her friend Zeb, an escapee from a place where zebras are imprisoned slaves. Claire learns that Castorman is also threatening to foreclose on Zeb's pasture. What will they ever do?

As the second act ends, Castorman has brought the bailiff to force Claire into concubinage and return Zeb to slavery, despite their tearful pleas for mercy.

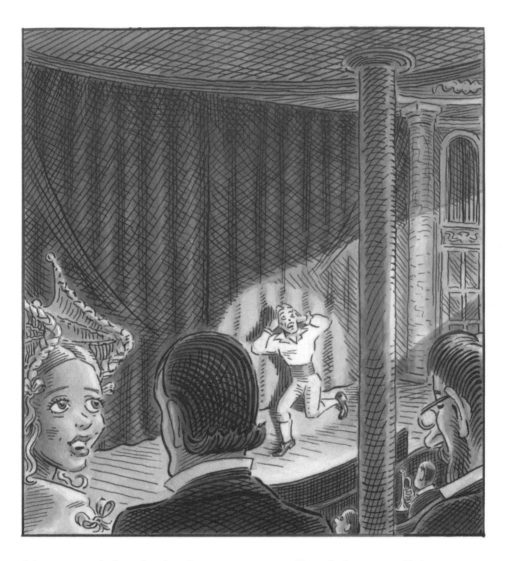

Johnny comes before the closed curtain in a state of horrified agitation. He has understood Claire's grave plight by lip-reading through his telescope. Charity, as a part-time teacher of the deaf, finds this a clever touch.

Displaying his rich baritone to great advantage, the actor playing Johnny sings,

To see the moonlings wildly cry,
My heart has lacerated,
A good man can't stand idly by,
Whilst crimes are perpetrated.

As Act III begins, Johnny has enlisted the help of his friend, Major Vaughan Brawn of the Royal Artillery. The major has built for Johnny a large version of a British military device called a "Congreve."

As the fuse on the Congreve slowly burns away, Vaughan Brawn sings a witty song about how the playwright of *The Way Of The World* also invented a way to get out of the world.

"Actually there were two different men, both named William Congreve," Locke whispers to Charity.

The moment the song ends, the fuse burns down, there is a terrific flash of lycopodium and Johnny vanishes from sight.

Johnny arrives on the Moon just in time to send Castorman and the bailiff hurtling into empty space as he sings,

Begone ye venal lunatics,
Take with you your depravity,
Alone I have the strength of six,
In lesser lunar gravity.

"My hero!" Claire exclaims.

"My hero, too," says Zeb.

"I hereby claim this land for England in the name of King William the Fourth!" says Johnny.

Claire and Zeb recoil in shock.

"We are not monarchists!" says Claire.

"We will not be a colony," says Zeb.

Embarrassed by his own presumption, Johnny quickly withdraws his claim.

In unison, Claire and Zeb shout, "We hereby claim ourselves for the United States of America in the name of President Andrew Jackson!"

"And the Moon shall be a free state," Zeb adds.

The show ends with a grand cakewalk as the entire cast sings,

Moonbeams falling from on high,
Will break the legislative tie,
Hurrah, huzzah, the moonbeams are a boon!

Twelve states slave and twelve states free,
Shamed the name of liberty,
Hurrah, huzzah, it was the way to ruin!

The future's incandescent,
Our bright new star's a crescent,
The flag's unfurled, the lunar world has joined our blessed Union,
Hurrah, huzzah, communion with the Moon!

Seeing Charity to her door after the theatre, Locke gives her a keepsake: a small rising sun emblem just like *The Sun*'s newsboys wear. Theirs are brass, but Locke has had this one stamped out of silver.

"Thank you, Richard," says Charity, calling him by his Christian name for the first time.

Two nights later, Locke and Charity ascend the stairs at 91 Spring Street for dinner at the home of Lorenzo Da Ponte.

Above his store, Da Ponte's daughter Maria serves as hostess. Her husband, the noted tenor Antonio Bagioli and their daughter Theresa, are at the table, as are two of Da Ponte's students, Dan Sickles and Phil Key, and boarders from Baltimore, Ed Poe and his cousin Virginia Clemm. Dinner is spaghetti with veal pulpetti in a spicy tomato sauce.

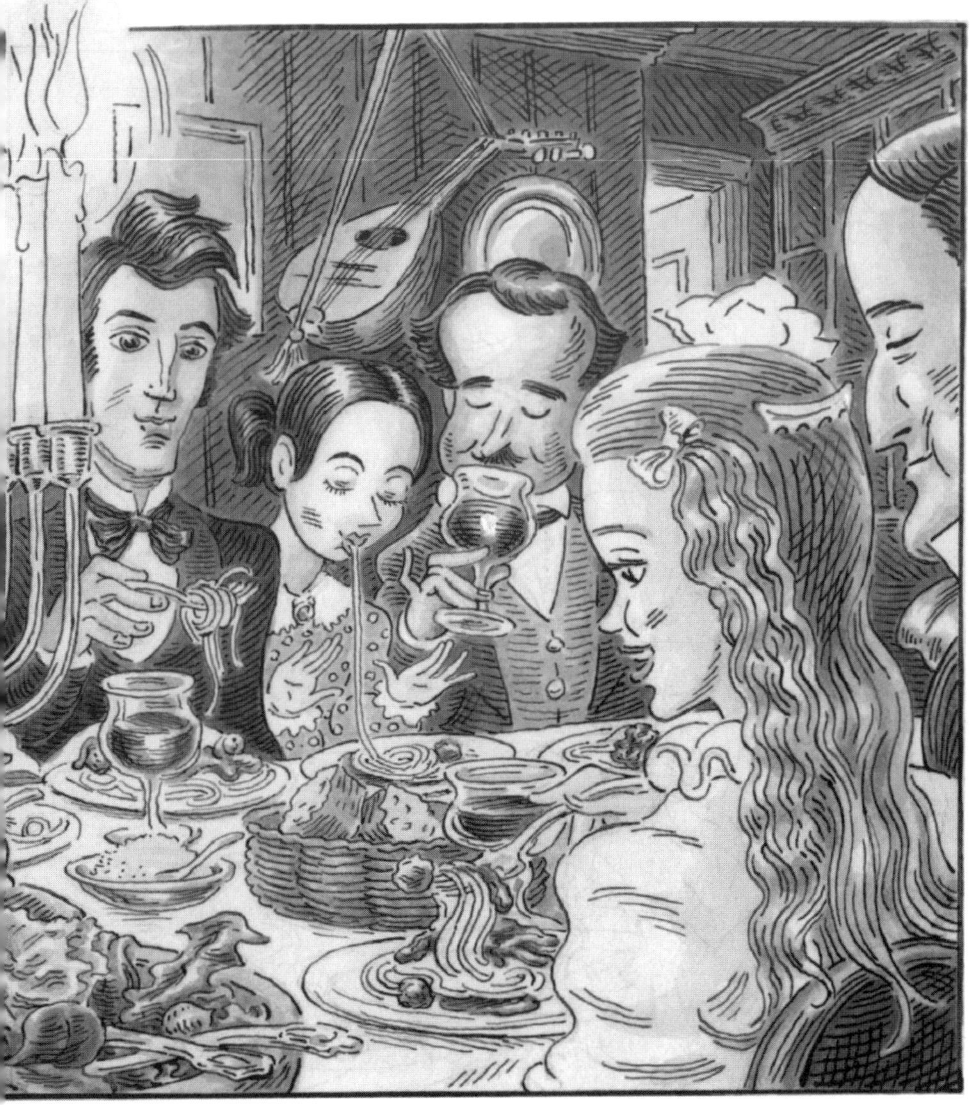

Maria and Antonio serenade the company with *La Ci Darem la Mano*, music by Mozart, lyrics by Da Ponte.

Locke toasts the couple's musical gifts and Maria's culinary talent. The spaghetti sauce contains the first tomatoes he has tasted.

He tells how he once, as a reporter, traveled to Salem, New Jersey where a certain
Colonel Johnson had promised to prove that tomatoes were not poisonous by eating
one on the courthouse steps. Flanked by his weeping wife and his personal physician,
Johnson took a big bite of one.

When the colonel failed to drop dead on the spot, the disappointed crowd pummeled Johnson, the wife, and the doctor with the ripe vegetables.

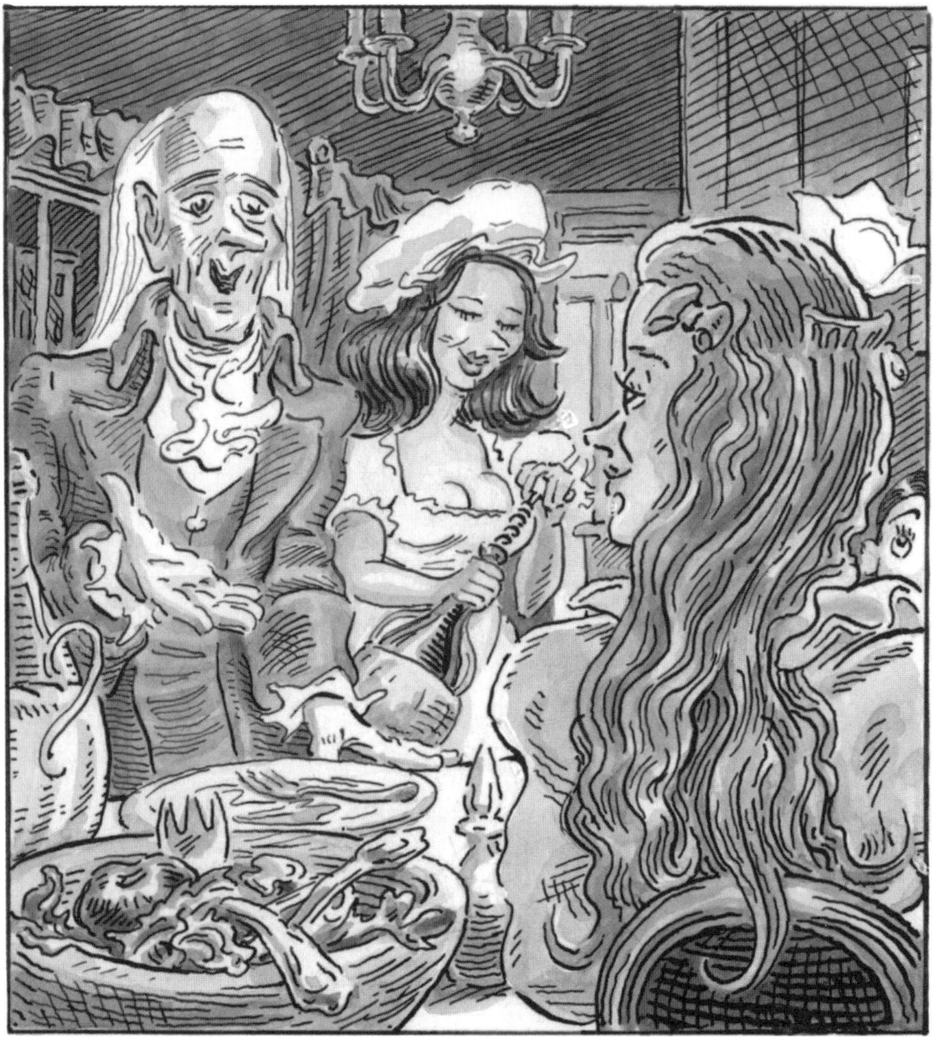

Da Ponte introduces Charity to the company as "the daughter of my estimable patron the Reverend Moore and, in her own right, a leading Wheatstone virtuoso." Charity is glad she hadn't thought to bring her concertina.

Da Ponte then says, "The ancient poet Lucian imagined going to the Moon in a boat carried up by a waterspout. Later, Cyrano de Bergerac dreamed of going there by wrapping himself with bottles of morning dew which the evaporative action of the Sun would lift. But only now, in modern times, do we finally know what really is on the Moon thanks to Doctor Herschel's marvelous telescope."

He offers a toast to Locke as "the man who brought New York the wonderful news of life on the Moon." Locke accepts the honor, but modestly mentions that *The Sun* had merely re-published material from the *Edinburgh Journal of Science*.

Phil Key improvises a parody of his father's well-known song:

Oh say can you see,
On the face of the Moon,
The idiot grin,
Of a cretin baboon

"I sure wish I could get my hands on one of those flying moongirls," says Dan Sickles. "Theresa, will you be my little moonmaid?" he says, tossing the baby into the air.

The baby falls to the floor and bites Sickles hard on the ankle.

"You fool!" says Key and punches Sickles.

"I'll kill you!" says Sickles, returning the blow.

The two run down to the street to continue their fight.

There is a long silence until Ed Poe rises unsteadily to his feet and says slowly, "Can I be the only man in this city who can see that this entire Moon report is nothing but a preposterous hoax?"

Locke starts to rise. "Sir, I beg your pardon," he says. Charity pulls him down, whispering, "The man is drunk, Richard. Let him speak."

Poe continues. "The story says this supposed telescope has a magnifying power of 50,000 times. The Moon is 250,000 miles away. So the telescope should show the Moon as it would appear from a distance of 5 miles. Now don't tell me anyone can spot a bird—even a large bird—from 5 miles away—let alone make out the color of its eyes. It's completely absurd. And Mr. Locke, I don't believe your tomato story either."

172

"I should accuse you of making the whole Moon story up if it weren't in fact a shameless plagiarism of a story I myself wrote for the *Southern Literary Messenger*."

"Not my usual reading," Locke murmurs to Charity.

Poe then recites his "Unparalleled Adventures of Hans Pfaall," It's about a Rotterdam bellows manufacturer whose business has fallen off due to the ready availability of cheap newspaper for kindling fires. To escape his creditors, Hans, the bellows man, uses his skills to construct a huge gas balloon that takes him to, of all places, the surface of the Moon. Except that it involves the Moon, the story is really not like the story in *The Sun* at all.

Rambling now, Poe denounces all such stories as mere "fictional science." True science is yet to come, he says, and when it does it will show what no one expects: that space and time, energy and matter are all equivalent and that the universe came into being through a singular explosion of something infinitesimally small. Then he passes out face down on the dining table.

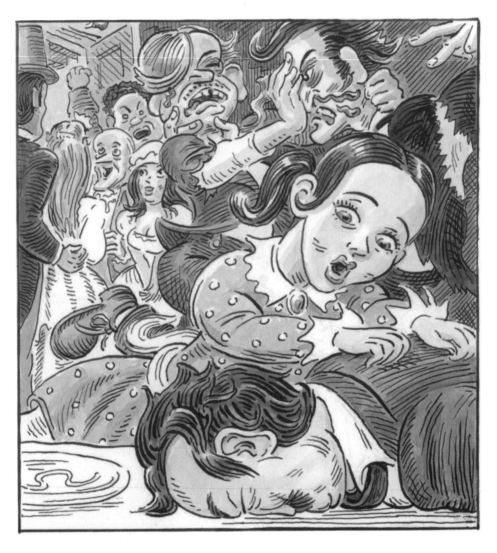

Key and Sickles return to the apartment bloodied and still fighting. Locke and Charity see it as a good time to thank Da Ponte and his family and make their farewells.

In the cab on the way back to Chelsea, Charity senses Locke's discomfiture.

"Pay no attention to what that Poe person said, Richard. He is obviously completely insane."

"Still, he's right about one thing," says Locke, "you couldn't see a bird if it were 5 miles away." Then, after a pause, he says. "Maybe 'a magnifying power of 50,000 times' was a misprint. Maybe it was more."

The next morning Locke has visitors in the offices of *The Sun*. Professors Olmsted, Loomis, and Silliman have come from Yale College. Their Dolland telescope is the biggest in America. With it they were the first to spot the return of Halley's Comet only months ago. But they have been unable to see any of Herschel's discoveries on the Moon. Would Mr. Locke be good enough to show them his copy of the *Edinburgh Journal of Science*?

Locke goes to the composing room to retrieve it. Fortune the typesetter has not come to work. Ben Day is filling in. Locke searches the place for the *Journal* in vain. Then he remembers, "I gave it to Audubon!" He must get it back immediately. Surely the Yale scientists will confirm its accuracy.

He explains to the professors what has happened. The *Journal* was left with the illustrator. The man lives in Harlem so it will take a while to go get it, but get it he shall. He leads the three men to the bar of Fraunces Tavern and tells the bartender to give them whatever they want and to put it on Ben Day's account. He tells them to wait for him and then he rushes off.

The steamboat up the Hudson would be too slow this time. He runs to the livery next to Niblo's and rents the fastest horse they have. Immediately he finds himself stalled in the heavy Broadway traffic.

Gradually, he makes his way to the sparsely settled countryside above Amity Street and goads the horse into a full gallop.

He gallops past the American Indian enclave known as Seneca Village.

He arrives at the Audubon house only to find it boarded up, with fresh wagon tracks leading away from it.

Luckily, Audubon and his wife have not gotten far. They tell Locke they are heading out west to see the California condor. Locke asks Audubon about the *Edinburgh Journal of Science*. Audubon thinks a minute and then says, "Ah yes, the great blue heron."

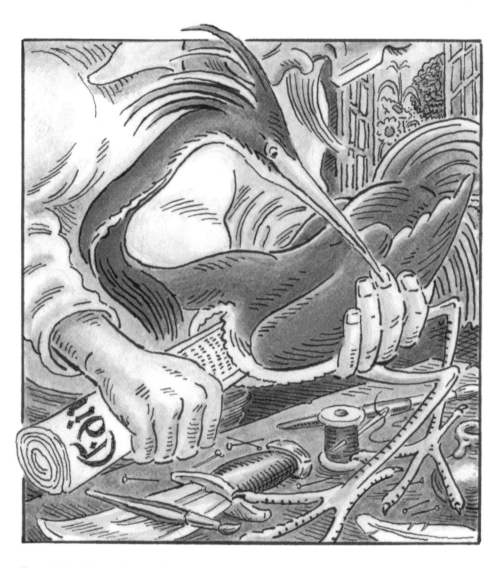

He explains that in his taxidermy work it is often necessary to stuff out the specimen with straw or old newspapers. "One of the better uses for newspaper," he adds. In the case of the great blue heron, the rolled *Journal* was a perfect fit for its abdomen. "I must have that paper back," says Locke impatiently.

"I'm afraid I already sold the bird, newspaper innards and all," says Audubon. Locke is aghast. "Sold it? To whom?" he says. "To a cheap Scotsman," says Audubon, "I was asking 12 dollars for it and he chiseled me down to 9." Unfortunately, Audubon has neither the name nor the location of the purchaser of the great blue heron. "And now the condor beckons," he says, slapping the reins as the wagon clanks away.

Locke is at a loss. Without the original *Journal* he'll be accused of making up the whole story. Well, at least Fortune the typesetter will remember me giving it to him to copy, he thinks. And I shall put an advertisement in the newspaper for the great blue heron. It will be terrible to disappoint the Yale professors for now, but there really is no choice. He urges the horse back toward the city.

As his horse is going at a good trot down a long downhill stretch of Broadway in the West 90s, Locke is passed by a boy happily mounted on a wooden contrivance with only two wheels. The frightened horse rears nearly throwing its rider.

Damned *draisienne*, Locke thinks. He has heard of these French machines but it is the first he's encountered. "Preposterous," he says aloud.

A mile or so down the road he sees the boy again, now sprawled on the road with the wreckage of his contraption. Pride goeth before a fall, Locke can't help thinking.

It is late afternoon when Locke arrives tired and dusty at Fraunces Tavern. The bartender tells him that Professors Olmsted and Loomis had to leave to catch a ship taking them somewhere across the Atlantic, but Professor Silliman is still here.

Having drunk six of the bar's special Manhattan Moonshine "cocktails," Silliman is staggering on top of a table singing a song about elm trees. Locke tries to tell him about the missing *Edinburgh Journal of Science*, but the man is nearly insensate. Locke puts him in a cab.

Understandably thirsty after his marathon on horseback, Locke finds himself standing at the bar next to his old friend Finbar Finn, a reporter for the *Herald*. Locke tells Finn about the Yale professors and the missing *Journal of Science*.

The next morning, Locke goes to the composing room to find Fortune has again not appeared for work. Ben Day is again setting the type himself. Locke tells him about the Yale professors and the missing *Journal*, and warns him about the charges the astronomers ran up on his bar tab. Then they compose an advertisement to run in every edition until it gets results.

SEEKING THE GREAT BLUE HERON
A taxidermied figure by Mr. Audubon
Notify Editor *The Sun*.   Reward

Locke questions Joey the newsboy. "Who was it who gave you that package on Canal Street?"

"A man," Joey says.

"What kind of man, Joey?"

"A man wearing a dress," says Joey. He describes the dress.

"A Scotsman!" says Locke. "Joey, find that Scotsman and bring him to me. There's a quarter dollar for you if you do."

A day later, and Fortune once again is absent. Locke must find out why. Suddenly, the air is shattered by a deafening noise. Joey has brought to the office a large bagpipe player. "Is this the man who gave you that package?" Locke asks Joey. "No," says Joey, "but he's a Scotsman."

Locke explains to Joey that not just any Scotsman will do, gives him ten cents for his efforts, and tells him to keep looking.

Locke goes to the home of Fortune the typesetter and makes a terrible discovery. Fortune is dead. His mangled body was found on Broome Street. There are no witnesses to what happened, but the neighbors rumor that he was trampled by a savage wild boar that had been seen in the area. Holding a wake are Fortune's widow Sara and young son Timothy. Lending comfort to the bereaved are the devout hairdresser Pierre Toussaint and Charity Moore. Locke would have been happier to see Charity again had the occasion not been so grim.

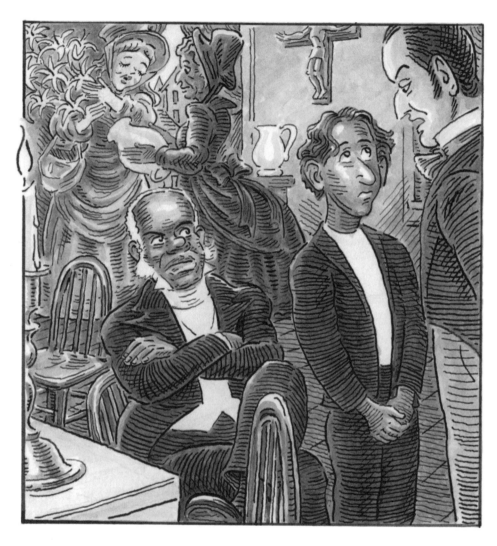

Charity tells Sara she can work for her as a ladies' maid at Chelsea. Locke offers Timothy a job at *The Sun*. "You can be a printer's devil," he says. The pious Pierre looks askance until Locke explains that the term merely refers to an apprentice in Timothy's father's profession.

Locke stops at the sentry box of Leatherhead Hays, the local constable. He asks him to investigate the death of Fortune and to keep an eye out for any mysterious Scotsmen or stuffed great blue herons. As is customary, he gives the man a few dollars.

A sobered Professor Silliman appears again at *The Sun* office. Locke tells him how his copy of the *Journal of Science* has gone missing, and promises to find it. Silliman tells him that Olmsted and Loomis are on their way to Cape Town to see the great John Herschel themselves, though the journey will take weeks.

Then *The Sun* receives a new shock. Still mourning the death of their fellow worker Fortune, the staff learns that Joey, the well-liked newsboy, has been found dead on Mercer Street, every bone in his body shattered. Again nobody heard or saw a thing. Again there are reports of a fierce boar nearly trampling people. It reminds Locke of how he met Charity.

Mortified by Joey's death, Locke goes to the spot where the child's body was found. It is in front of a shop offering articles made of caoutchouc, a form of South American tree sap. Locke enters the shop and is nearly overpowered by its horrific smell.

The proprietor of the shop, a Mr. Goodyear, tells him he is developing a process to make the unstable natural caoutchouc into something permanent. He shows him some of his products: a little pink thing he calls a "mistake remover." It is a popular item. "As long as people keep making mistakes," he says, "I will be in business."

"And this little item I call a 'mistake preventer,'" Goodyear says dangling a tubular object in front of him. Thinking of the legions of parentless, homeless children like Joey in the city, Locke understands. "Do you sell many of those?" Locke asks. Goodyear admits to having only one customer for the preventers.

Locke buys a remover and a preventer for a total of 10 cents and then asks Goodyear if he can shed any light on Joey's death and if he's seen any Scotsmen around. "I did sell a quantity of caoutchouc to a coat-maker named Mackintosh once, but that was years ago," Goodyear says, adding, "I'm sorry about your newsboy."

The newsboys and newsgirls have gathered to plan a municipal boar hunt to avenge the death of Joey. Timothy Fortune joins them. One of the boys, the enterprising Billy Tweed, has a bundle of lethally sharpened sticks that he distributes to the children for a penny apiece. They take an oath to find and destroy the wild boar, whom they have named Napoleon.

The children spread out to find Napoleon. Fetching his old cavalry saber, Locke joins one group heading up Church Street. When they find a mild old wandering sow, Locke pleads for her life as a "poor fellow creature who could never hurt anyone." "Aw, let us kill it," the kids yell, but Locke dissuades them.

As the boar hunters continue to swarm through the streets, the day begins to darken. It is too early for sunset. Locke looks up to see the onset of an eclipse of the sun. He stops in his tracks to watch.

Just before the moment of totality, he sees far off in the crowd a man in a tam-o'shanter. But when the darkness begins to lift as the Moon uncovers the sun, the Scotsman has vanished.

Meanwhile, by torchlight, in an alley called Jersey Street, the group of children with Timothy Fortune corner and stab to death the large and dreadful Napoleon.

The next Sunday morning finds Locke in St. Peter's Episcopal Church, saying a silent prayer for the souls of Fortune and Joey. Just in case God exists, he thinks. He is there to report, as he had promised, on Clement Moore's sermon, in which the reverend doctor expounds on his theory that the people on the moon probably speak Hebrew and could be communicated with by semaphore and giant letters laid out in coal on the prairie. He takes down the whole oration in shorthand.

Charity is also present, and Locke and she exchange glances.

Moore's sermon in its entirety appears in Tuesday's edition of *The Sun*. On the same day, the *New York Herald* leads with, "It has come to our attention that the story in *The Sun* about new discoveries on the moon is nothing but a complete and shameless fabrication perpetrated by its editor, Mr. Richard Locke, who in addition to a total disregard for truth has expert knowledge of telescopes." The byline on the article is Finbar Finn. Ben Day receives a one word personal note from James Gordon Bennett: "Ha!"

Locke runs to Fraunces Tavern certain he'll find Finn there, and he does. "You swine," he says, "Are you out to destroy me? I never told you any of that!" "Bennett always says, 'Many a good story has been ruined by over-verification'," says Finn, "You made up a story, I made up a story." "I made up nothing," says Locke, "and where did you get the part about my being a telescope expert?"

"Remember when we both reported on the murder of the sea Captain Jacoby?" says Finn. "The man that I deduced had been bashed over the head with his own telescope?" says Locke. "I rest my case," says Finn. Finn has had too much to drink and in a short time so has Locke.

Locke arrives for work the next day severely hung over. Sara Fortune arrives with a letter for him from Charity Moore:

Richard, how could you? Father is furious. You've turned him into a laughingstock. From this moment I never want to have anything to do with you again.

"You certainly fooled me," says Ben Day. "Of course, we'll never run a retraction, but meanwhile *The Sun* cannot afford to have as its editor a notorious liar." Locke protests, but to no avail. "You're fired," says Day.

Locke goes home. In a fury, he smokes all the free cigars Ben Day has given him over the years and becomes violently ill. In his distress he thinks, how could this have happened? If the moon story is indeed a hoax, surely he is its greatest victim. But why? He believed the *Edinburgh Journal of Science*, but now his witnesses, Joey and Fortune, are dead, Audubon has gone west and the *Journal* is lost in some missing stuffed bird. He falls into a fitful sleep and dreams that a great blue heron is tearing his guts out.

When he ventures into the street a day later, he discovers the mood of the city has changed. People who were formerly enchanted by the moon story are now angry at having been duped. A group of children give him the raspberry and call him "Moonman" and "Moonie."

He goes to the sentry box, finds it empty, and hears that Constable Hays has been killed. Could there be another vicious wild pig? Can pigs climb stairs?

Hays' crushed body was found on a nearby roof.

Locke goes to Fraunces Tavern and starts to drink heavily. There he is accosted by Ed Poe. "Wasn't I the first to say that moon story was a hoax?" Poe drunkenly gloats. "Maybe it was," says Locke, "but I wasn't the one who made it up." He tells Poe about the missing *Journal* and the horrible deaths of Fortune, Joey, and the constable.

"Highly mysterious. Are you sure you're not the one who killed them all?" Poe asks with a smirk. Locke wishes he could kill Poe.

At his rooming house, he is confronted by his landlady. "This is a respectable house, Mr. Locke," she says, "not a place for lying scribblers. I'm afraid I must ask you to leave." He packs his few possessions in a bag and clears out.

Before long, Locke has drunk up his meager savings, had his bag stolen, and lost his hat and coat. He has taken to sleeping in doorways and asking passers-by for alms. And the weather has become chilly.

One morning, he awakens next to a pile of coal in a tiny windowless stone-walled room. For a few moments, he thinks he must have actually arrived in hell, and attempts a review of all his sins. "Well, awake at last," says a fat woman who suddenly appears with a bucket of water.

"Mrs. Satan?" says Locke.

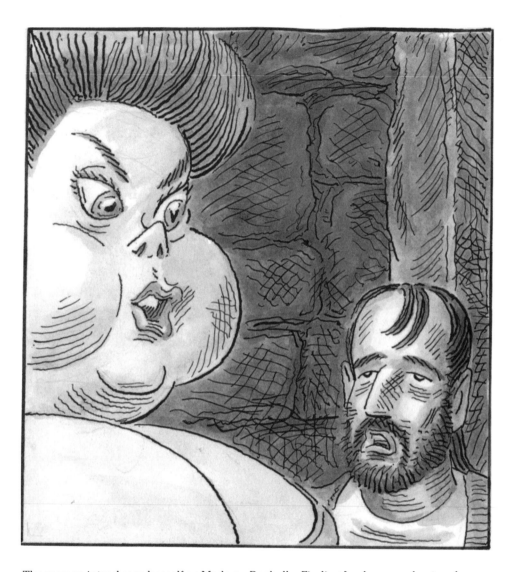

The woman introduces herself as Madame Rochelle. Finding Locke passed out on her doorstep, she has dragged him into the safety of her coal bin. "I could see you had once been a fine gentleman," she says, "and I took pity on you." Locke thanks her and introduces himself. He gives her an abbreviated version of his tale of woe. Although Rochelle admits to not reading much, she has heard of the moon story and has a one-word comment: "Bullshit."

"You can stay here if you like," Rochelle tells Locke. "I'll even feed you from time to time. All I ask is that you stoke the furnace and do a few other odd jobs around the whorehouse." Handing him the bucket of water, a razor, and some soap, she says, "Clean yourself up a bit and come upstairs and meet the family."

"Look what I found," says Rochelle to the crew of girls gathered around the kitchen table. The pork and beans they are sharing is the first decent meal Locke has had in days. He is offered beer, but turns it down saying, "I'd better not."

Madame Rochelle's on Greene Street is a popular and well-run establishment. Locke stokes the furnace when needed, sweeps the floors, and throws out the occasional unruly customer. The only really disagreeable task he must perform is the regular washing out of the house's used "preventers."

When he has gotten back his strength, he takes up Rochelle's offer of "the specialty of the house," her own buxom self, on her condition that he is not allowed to mess with any of the other girls.

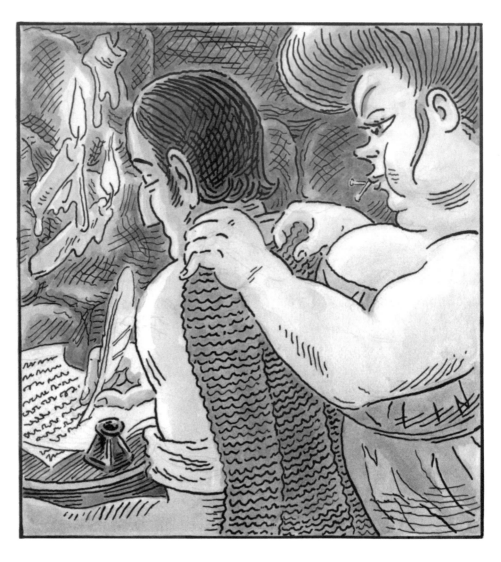

One evening, he feels well enough to sit down with paper and pen and start to write. Very well, he thinks, if the world chooses to take me as a writer of hoaxes, I shall write a hoax.

His story is titled *The Lost Manuscript of Mungo Park*. Mungo Park was a Scottish explorer who disappeared while tracing the course of the Niger River in Africa. He traveled with two slaves, Johnson and Demba, and a large quantity of oatmeal and whisky. They were last seen in 1806. Locke will tell what happened afterward, in the form of Park's first person narrative.

Park tells how the natives of the region are terrorized by the mokele-mbembe, an immense, man-eating, lizard-like animal of a kind known elsewhere only from fossilized remains. The natives appease the creature by sacrificing to it their most beautiful daughters.

Park encounters the mokele-mbembe, kills it with his trusty knobkerry, frees the girl, and is celebrated by the locals as a kind of god. Married to the girl he has saved, he lives the life of a king deep in the heart of the Dark Continent. Locke takes pleasure in writing the story. He is sure it is the best thing he has ever done.

For the first time in days, he ventures out of Madame Rochelle's. He brings *The Lost Manuscript of Mungo Park* to the dreaded James Gordon Bennett of the *Herald*, saying, "I have finally written a genuine hoax." Bennett looks it over.

"You know," says Bennett handing it back to him, "I was convinced you wrote the moon story, which, despite being a pack of lies, had its undeniable charms. Now I've changed my mind. This *Manuscript* tells me one thing: you are no writer. It stinks." Crestfallen, Locke leaves.

Phineas Barnum has come back to New York. He is showing Joice Heth at Niblo's again, or rather her embalmed corpse.

Also on display is a golden locket found among her personal effects. It contains a miniature portrait of the young George Washington with the inscription "To my beloved Mommy from Georgie." Perhaps young George didn't know how to spell "mammy," but the thought that the first president's mother may actually have been an enslaved black woman thrills the abolitionists, and the mummified mommy-mammy brings in a lot of business for Barnum.

At Chelsea, Clement Moore has been brooding. He has not overcome the embarrassment of having endorsed the moon hoax with his plan for human-batman communication. Also, his investment in the coal business has proven less profitable than he expected. Although he is widely known to have written *The Night Before Christmas*, it has never been published with his name attached. Now he will remedy that.

His new signed edition of the poem will subtly encourage parents to punish bad children with pieces of coal instead of gifts, thus boosting sales of the commodity. The poem now contains the lines:

> *A bundle of toys he had flung on his back,*
> *And some greasy black coal in a filthy old sack.*
> And: *The good children's stockings he filled with toys biggish,*
> *But nothing but coal for the nasty and piggish.*

He shows the new version to Charity who suggests he think it over for a while before making it public.

One afternoon, while sweeping the floors at Madame Rochelle's, Locke hears riotous laughter coming from one of the rooms. It has been a long time since he has had a good laugh. He opens the door a little and sees a naked old man entertaining five girls in various states of *deshabille*.

It is Lorenzo Da Ponte. Spotting him at the door, Da Ponte says, "Come in, Mr. Locke."

Da Ponte is telling the women a tale of his good friend, Giacomo Casanova, who hoodwinked a rich old woman into exchanging a large sum of money for a vial of "magical youth cream." Casanova's method was to show a withered crone applying the cream, and then sending her behind a screen whence emerged an identically dressed beauty of about sixteen years of age. Da Ponte acts out the scene with various hilarious voices. The girls are beside themselves with merriment and Locke gets to laugh the laugh he'd been craving.

Later, in Rochelle's kitchen, Locke and Da Ponte chat over coffee. "How is it," Locke asks, "that a reprobate like yourself has acquired the patronage of an absurdly upright reverend like Clement Moore?" "It's a long story," says Da Ponte. "I've got nothing but time," says Locke.

"I'm nearly ninety years old," says Da Ponte, "and I've had many careers. Long ago, I owned and operated a distillery in Sunbury, Pennsylvania, and drove around the countryside distributing my product. One snowy evening, I pulled up my wagon before a large house in Poughkeepsie, New York, and was asked in by its owner, a Major Henry Livingston."

"It was Christmas Eve and Livingston invited me to celebrate with his family. There was wonderful food and drink, several handsome children, dogs, cats, and music. It may have been the happiest gathering I've ever witnessed. When he learned that I had once known the great Mozart, Livingston offered to buy a barrel of my liquor. I told him he could have it gratis in exchange for his marvelous hospitality."

"After dinner was over, Livingston stood at the head of the table to read a poem he had just composed. *'Twas the night before Christmas,* it began, *and all through the house...*" "No!" says Locke. "Yes," says Da Ponte. "He wrote it. So you can imagine my surprise years later when I came to New York and first met the Reverend Moore in a bookstore and he told me he was the author of the poem. I told him he was mistaken and that I had been present when Major Henry Livingston first gave it to the world."

"What was Moore's reaction?" Locke asks. "He asked me how I would like it if he made me a professor of Italian at Columbia College." "Just for keeping quiet about the poem?" says Locke. "What a stroke of luck for me," says Da Ponte, "although I suppose the secret is out now." "I'll never tell," says Locke.

Just then, Madame Rochelle walks in. With her is, of all people, Charity Moore. Charity greets Da Ponte and then frowns when she sees Locke. She has come to give Rochelle her house's monthly consignment of Mr. Goodyear's "preventers." As an act of personal philanthropy Charity has made it one of her goals to see that the city's brothels are well supplied with the devices.

Suddenly, they all hear a great commotion in the street—shouts, screams, hoofbeats, and the clanging of bells. They run out to see that the whole city below Canal Street is on fire. All able-bodied men run to help fight the fire. They include Locke and Charity's driver. Charity will have to stay the night at Madame Rochelle's.

Fire-fighting companies at this time are private social organizations. As the city blazes, the fire companies take time out to fight each other.

The next afternoon, the fire is out and much of the city, which consisted largely of wooden buildings, is in smoldering ruins. There are many dead. Crowds of people, including Locke and Charity, walk downtown to view the damage. As they walk, Locke tells Charity about the lost copy of the *Edinburgh Journal of Science*. He swears he never made up the moon story and is sorry for the embarrassment it caused her father. He points out that he himself is the only real victim of the hoax and that it has effectively ruined him.

They reach the spot on William Street where *The Sun*'s offices once stood. The steam-powered iron printing press has survived the fire, but little else. Then Locke notices a damp, charred envelope among the ashes. It is marked, "To the Editor, *The New York Sun*." Locke tears it open.

Locke's newspaper advertisement has been answered. The letter simply states, "I have the blue bird," and is signed, "Samuel Morey, Orford, New Hampshire."

As they walk back toward Greene Street, Locke explains how Audubon put the *Journal* inside his great blue heron and then sold it. If this Morey person in fact has it, and if Locke can get it back into his own hands, he can show the world he is no lying, hoax-writing fabulist, but merely a stupendously gullible fool. "That would be better," says Charity. It is mid-December and snow has begun to fall.

Locke's tale has touched Charity Moore's heart. She had liked the man. The idea that he had invented a bogus newspaper story had disappointed her terribly. Her father's shame at falling for the yarn made her feel even worse. Perhaps she could help.

The fire and the snow have brought New York to a standstill. Charity suggests to Locke that they go to Orford, New Hampshire to retrieve the missing Journal. Madame Rochelle is sympathetic and gives Locke a few dollars to make the trip.

They hire a coach and soon are traveling through the wintry landscape into the north country.

In Cape Town, South Africa, it is summer. The Yale astronomers Olmsted and Loomis have arrived to meet the great John Herschel, who has continued his long study and cataloging of the stars of the southern hemisphere. The visitors present him with the pamphlet version of *The Sun*'s "Great Astronomical Discoveries." Herschel reads it slowly and then laughs heartily. "It is too bad my real discoveries here won't be that exciting," he says.

The roads are rough and often clogged with snow as Locke and Charity ride onward
in the coach. The weather is cold, and although the coach is supplied with rugs and
blankets, the couple sit close together and begin to embrace each other for warmth.
After a while of this they kiss, and then they succumb to something more than a chaste
embrace. When it is over, Charity's unusually cool hand is warm as she strokes Locke's
head and says, "Richard, you are going bald."

They arrive at the city of Hartford, Connecticut and spend the night at an inn, J. Carter's Strangers Resort.

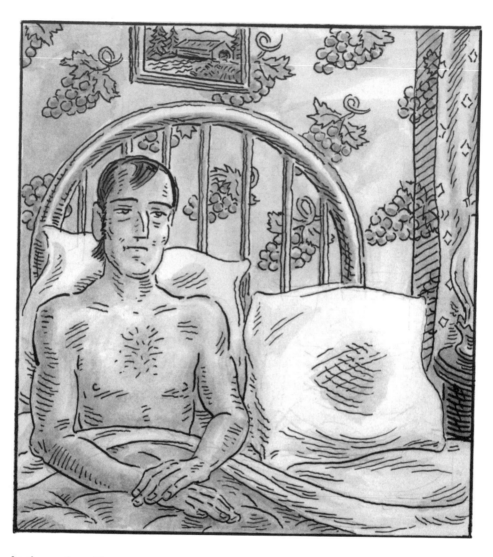

Locke awakens the next morning and is distressed to find Charity gone.

After a while, Charity returns. She has been shopping in Hartford. She has bought them matching hats made of the striped fur of the raccoon. They put them on and look into a mirror. "Don't we make a fine couple of frontier explorers?" Charity says. Locke feels silly.

They will make the next part of their journey in a one-horse open sleigh. The sleigh glides northward through the increasingly hilly snow-covered territory.

At length, they arrive in Orford, New Hampshire, and find the farmstead of Samuel Morey—a house with a pigsty in the front yard, a barn, and several attached and free-standing sheds and outbuildings.

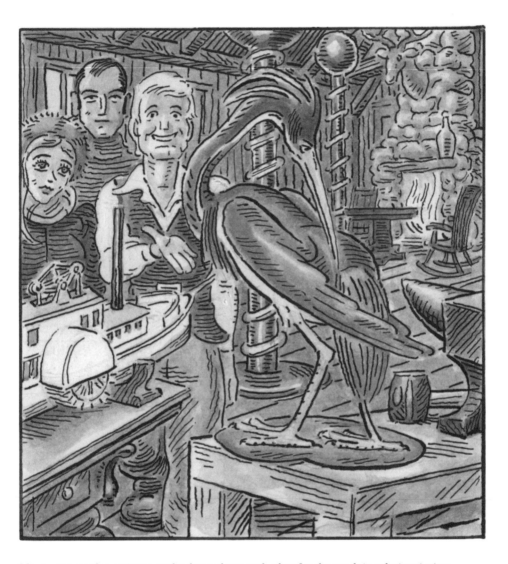

Morey greets the visitors at the front door and, after Locke explains their mission, invites him and Charity in. A fire is going in the hearth. Morey is evidently some kind of rural tinkerer. There are tools of many sorts, a cunning model of a steamboat, odd-looking equipment, and, on a workbench, the stuffed figure of a great blue heron. "It was given to me by an acquaintance who has an affinity for birds," says Morey.

"We'd like to buy that bird," says Locke. "It'll cost you ten dollars." Says Morey. Charity takes the money out of her bag and hands it to the man.

Using his penknife, Locke carefully cuts open the bird's breast. There, rolled into a tube is the long sought *Edinburgh Journal of Science*. Charity is delighted—and a bit relieved to find there really is such a thing. "Aha," says Locke, "I swore to you I didn't make it up. This proves it."

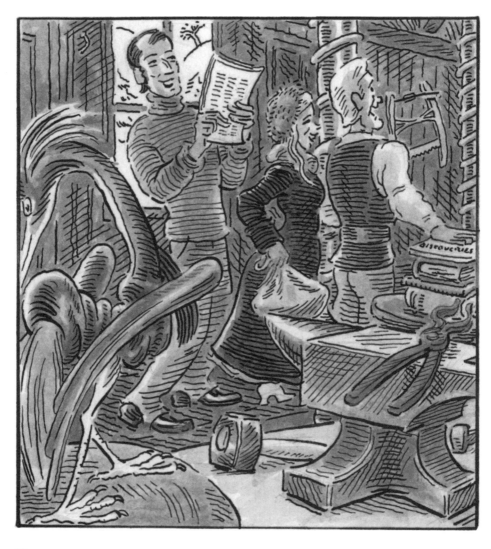

"You may keep the bird," says Locke to Morey. "This is all I wanted." He laughs. They all laugh. Morey knows the moon story and has a copy of *The Sun*'s pamphlet version. "Happy to have been of service," says Morey.

Morey invites Charity and Locke to a light repast of ham that he has personally smoked, and tea. With the snow outside, the fire brightly crackling, the excellent ham, the hot tea, good company, and the lost *Journal* found, it is a serene moment.

Leaning back in his chair, Locke notices a heavy-looking iron object hanging by chains from the rafters, and asks Samuel Morey about it.

"Ah, the vapor engine," says Morey, "one of my inventions. A means of propulsion powered by the internal combustion of a liquid."

He describes a device utilizing his engine. He calls it the "autovehicule." The autovehicule is completely self-propelled. "It might make horses go extinct," says Morey, "but that's the horses' problem." The autovehicule would be fast, strong and reliable, and everyone on Earth would be able to have one.

Morey describes a future when the countryside is crisscrossed by smooth roadways over which millions of autovehicules course night and day, greatly enriching and accelerating everyday life for all mankind.

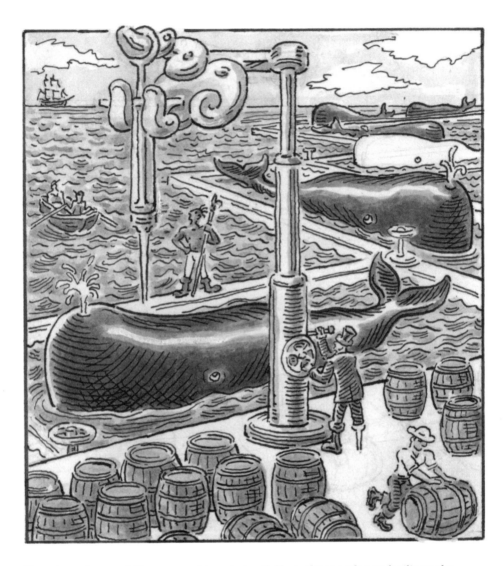

Morey's engine would be powered by whale oil. He outlines a plan to facilitate the production of fuel by the domestication of the sperm whale. The whales would be bred and kept in pens, and their oil extracted from their heads as needed with little pain or inconvenience to the great animals.

Locke and Charity are captivated by the man's vivid imagination. "When will all this become reality?" Locke asks. "Never," says Morey. "I sold all my rights and patents to a certain Mr. Peter Cooper of New York, who immediately suppressed the whole idea so it wouldn't conflict with his infernal 'railroad' scheme." Locke remembers his smoky, lurching, spark and cinder-flecked demonstration ride on the nation's first and only "railway"—extending a full 13 miles out of Baltimore and taking hours to traverse them. "That's too bad," says Charity.

"But I do have one working model of the autovehicule," says Morey. "Would you like to see it?" They say they would. They put on their warm clothing and Morey leads them to a rustic shed outside. He opens the shed door, revealing the autovehicule standing among bales of hay. It resembles a large overturned vat with windows and doors and is painted a glossy black. It sits upon four fat-looking black wheels.

Locke prods one of the wheels gently with his foot and it indents slightly. "Caoutchouc?" says Locke. "Gesundheit," says Morey and then, "Yes, caoutchouc indeed. If that idiot Goodyear ever figures out it needs to be mixed with sulfur, he might really have something."

Morey opens the doors of the autovehicule and says, "Hop in," and they do. Morey sits before something that looks like a ship's wheel. Locke and Charity sit on a well-upholstered loveseat behind him. Morey turns a key and the device, after emitting a coughing noise, commences a soft, purring, continuous hum. He releases a catch and a music box appears tinkling Mozart's *Rondo Alla Turca*.

The autovehicule starts to roll forward slowly down a sloping, snow-covered woodland path until it comes to the edge of a frozen lake.

Then it leaps forward and soon it is hurtling across the lake at great speed.

Locke and Charity clutch each other in terror.

As it approaches the other side of the lake, the autovehicule slows slightly, then makes an about-turn and traverses the lake again. And again and again. Locke and Charity regain their composure and realize they love the thrilling, gliding sensation of being inside the moving autovehicule.

Then Morey takes them round and round the perimeter of the lake, going faster and faster with each circuit. Then he turns quickly toward the middle of the lake and brings the conveyance to an abrupt halt. Then he demonstrates that it can go backward as well as forwards. "Would you like to try it?" he asks Locke.

After a few brief instructions, Locke takes the wheel and soon is circling the lake as quickly as Morey had. He thinks it is a delightful experience unlike anything he has known.

Without asking Morey, Locke invites Charity to try running the autovehicule herself, and she does, alternately giggling and shrieking with joy as they spin merrily along.

All at once, the air is torn by a terrific noise like a thunderclap. The ice beneath them is cracking. "Jump!" Morey yells, and they all manage to leap to safety just in time to see the autovehicule disappear into the frigid, black depths of the lake.

In silence, they trudge back through the snow to Morey's house. After his autovehicule ride, Locke can't help thinking, my God, what a slow and tedious process walking is.

As they huddle around Morey's hearth, Charity says, "I'm so sorry, sir. It must have been something I did wrong with your marvelous machine." "Nonsense, child. The ice broke, that's all," says Morey. "But if only we hadn't asked to see it, you'd still have your wonderful autovehicule," says Locke. "Never mind," says Morey, "it was obsolete anyway."

"You see," says Morey, "the physical world is like this fruitcake," putting that confection along with some hot spiced tea on a table for his guests. "The atoms that make up all things are like the nuts, raisins and candied fruit that are suspended here in a matrix of brandy-soaked cake. Except that in the case of the atoms, the matrix is empty and invisible—a perfect vacuum. But I have discovered that the vacuum in fact contains more power than anything else in the universe. To put it briefly: there ain't no nothing! I have devised a means to harness that power and I have patented it."

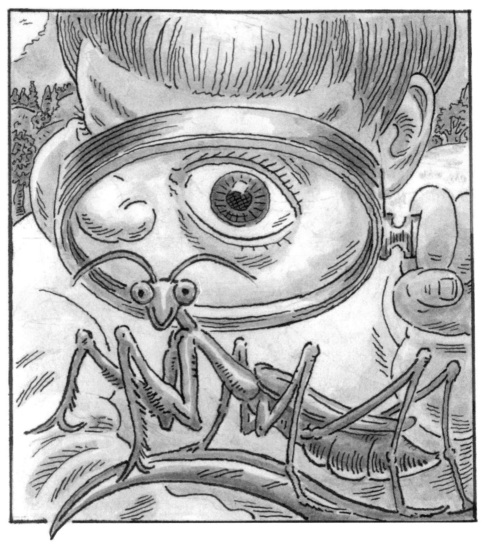

"Since I was a boy, I have been endowed, or shall I say afflicted, with a great curiosity. I had a magnifying glass that enabled me to see the intricate detail with which all things were put together. When I learned that at bottom all things were separated from each other and even from the parts of themselves by a sheer nothingness, I could not accept it."

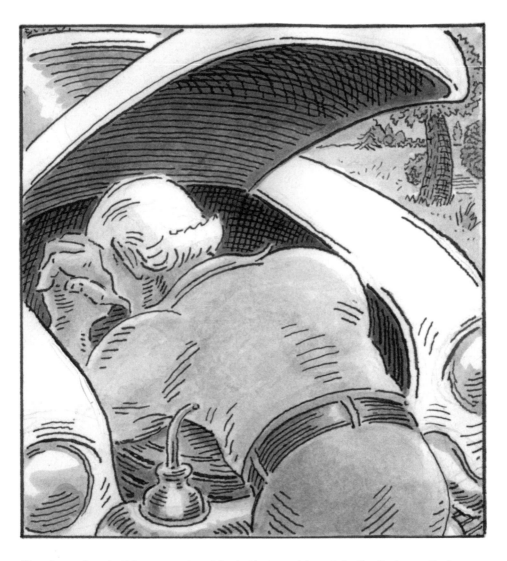

"I undertook to build a new autovehicule that would contain the first practical version of my vacuum engine. It was large. I painted it white. I called it the Albino. Powered by energy-packed nothingness, the engine would generate a force vastly greater than gravity."

"I started it up. Rather than budging, it just settled a few inches into the ground beneath it. I had foolishly installed the engine upside down, an easy thing to correct. After a bit of tinkering, it worked just fine."

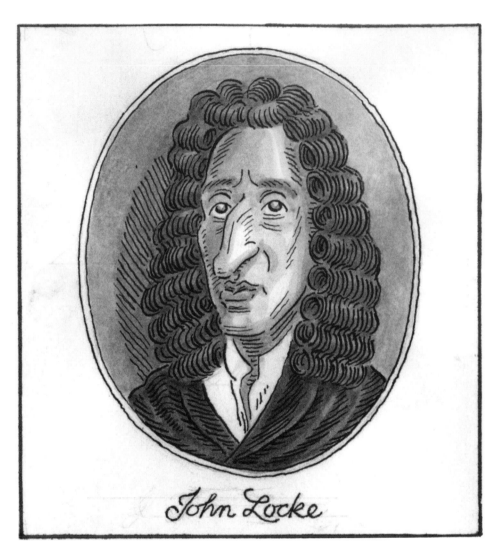

John Locke

"You can imagine my elation. The British philosopher John Locke asserted that we can only know anything by direct sense experience. An ancestor of yours, Mr. Locke?" "My great-great-grandfather," says Richard Locke.

"Now I could go anywhere and experience everything," Morey continues, "and as I said, my curiosity was boundless."

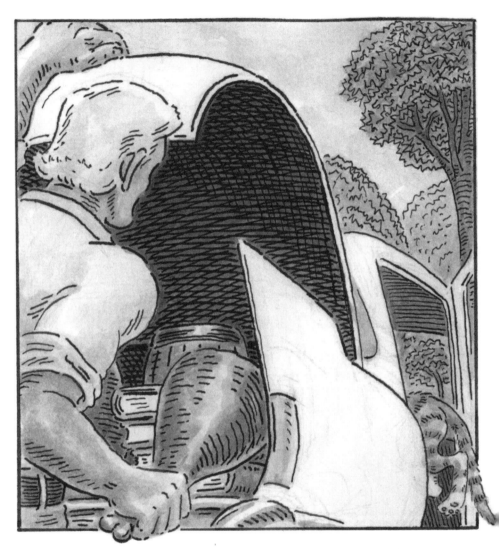

"I set out to see the world. I packed the Albino with a few tools, a few books, some clothing, a cask of water and a large smoked ham. At the last moment my old tabby cat jumped into the back seat."

"The Albino rose slowly off the ground and gradually gained speed. Before long, I was high above the Connecticut River, following it like a blue ribbon on its course toward the sea."

"Soon, I was over the Atlantic Ocean. If I rose high enough, the Earth below functioned well as a map of itself."

"I headed toward Ireland, where my ancestors came from, slowed down, and swooped low over it, saw some poor folk and sheep among thatched sod houses, and extensive plantings of what looked like potatoes."

"I circled the domes of both Saint Paul's Cathedral in London and Saint Peter's in Rome in the course of just a few minutes."

"Then I headed east, straight across the Mediterranean toward Egypt, where I was able to get a close look at the Sphinx and the pyramids."

"I guided the Albino ever eastward, seeing and smelling the Ganges River, then soaring upward over the Himalayas, and then following the Great Wall of China its entire length."

"Next, I turned south and west. At a low altitude, I traversed the equatorial jungle of Africa. I thought for a moment I glimpsed a giant reptile among the trees, but it was time to move on."

"I crossed the Atlantic for the second time that day as I headed for Brazil, where I followed the Amazon to its headwaters."

"There I took a sharp left turn and pointed the Albino toward Antarctica, greatly discomfiting a flock of penguins when I got there."

"Now turning northward over the Pacific Ocean, I was soon at the North Pole, the land of the polar bear, but I saw no sign of Saint Nicholas."

"Then I crossed the entire North American continent, the majestic purple Rockies, the amber waves of grain, the Mississippi, the fruited plain."

Locke and Charity can't believe anything they are hearing. Fruitcake power indeed, Locke thinks to himself.

Morey continues: "Arriving again at the Atlantic, I had a good idea. I tilted the Albino downward and plunged deep into the sea where I was able to witness the mating ritual of the sperm whale."

"As I emerged from the sea, night had fallen. Directly ahead of me was a splendid full moon high in the sky. Well, why not? I thought."

"Before long, I was near enough to the moon to see it in great detail. Believe me, there is nothing more bleak than its gray, crater-pocked, dusty surface."

"Then I noticed a strange thing," says Morey. "Near the Mare Imbrium, I saw what appeared to be a wisp of vaporous matter. As I guided the Albino closer to it, I could see that the vapor arose from a great, cloud-covered basin."

"As I dropped lower, below the clouds now, I saw a patch of brilliant poppies growing on the crater edge, and then an interior wall of immense crystals gleaming like diamonds, and then a forest bordering on a smooth lake in the middle of which the clouds and rivers were emerging from a glowing mountaintop."

"You!" Locke and Charity exclaim simultaneously. "Yes," says Morey, "Yours truly. I was there."

Morey goes on with his tale. "I flew low and slowly over the green hills at the base of the mountain and was astonished to see the extraordinary wildlife, the bison, the giant beaver, the sheep, the pelicans, the zebras, the amazing unicorns. I gently set the Albino down alongside a sparkling brook."

"The moment I opened the door, the cat jumped out and ran away. I never saw that animal again. I gazed about and then stood in complete, thunderstruck awe. Here was an island of beauty that no one else could possibly know existed."

"Then I heard a soft whooshing sound overhead. I looked up to see a veritable flock of naked flying people descending onto the grass around me. Their wings weren't like feathery angel wings one sees in paintings—more like those of the bat, but of course much larger. The natives of this place had discovered me, and were chattering vigorously in their incomprehensible tongue."

"By means of hand signs and pantomime, I indicated my peaceful intentions and they returned the sentiment with smiles and gestures."

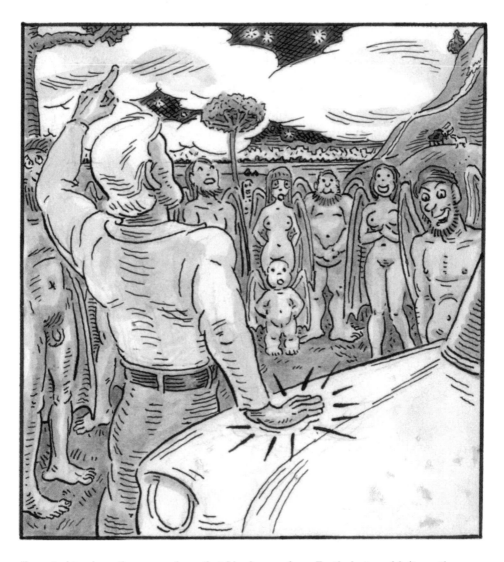

"I wanted to show them somehow that I had come from Earth, but couldn't see the planet in the small patches of sky visible through the cloud cover. To emphasize that the Albino had carried me there, I slapped the vehicle affectionately on the fender, which gave out a loud gong-like sound."

"Immediately, the moonpeople were all slapping the fenders and evidently taking pleasure in the sound, with some even humming in harmony with it. Later I learned that this was their first contact with an object made of metal of any kind. Apart from that noise, the moonpeople seemed little interested in the Albino."

"They brought me grapes and bananas and examples of other kinds of fruit I had never seen before. I gave them slices of my ham, which they liked well. We had a fine picnic, washed down with water from that lovely lunar brook."

"One pretty young moonwoman seemed to take a special interest in me. Pointing at her chest with her thumb, she said, 'Yaffa,' which I took to be her name. I pointed at myself and said, 'Sam.' Yaffa said 'Sam,' then, 'Sam, Sam, Sam.' I said 'Yaffa, Yaffa, Yaffa.' I was now on first-name terms with an inhabitant of another world."

"By means of gestures and facial expressions, Yaffa conveyed to me her pity for the fact that I had no wings. She found my clothing to be a source of amusement, evidently having no prior experience with the concept. With a deft move, she peeled off my shirt and closely inspected my back, thinking perhaps that my wings just hadn't started to sprout. Then she pouted and said, 'Sam, Sam, Sam.' For my part, I was happy to learn that curiosity also existed on the moon."

"The day on the moon is 14 times as long as a day on Earth. During that first day, it became evident that Yaffa had made it a personal project to bring me up to moon standards. I found that, due to the moon's lesser gravity, I was able to jump extraordinarily high. Yaffa wasn't impressed."

"She fashioned artificial wings for me out of banana leaves, thinking they might help me fly, but they didn't. Although she laughed at me, she showed affection for me in other ways that didn't make me feel like a disabled person."

"Gradually, Yaffa began to teach me the rudiments of the moon language. I was helped greatly by one of the books I had taken along, *The Compendious Lexicon of the Hebrew Language*, written by your father, I believe, Miss Moore."

"Father would be so happy to know that," says Charity. "And I taught Yaffa a bit of English," Morey adds.

"The people called themselves the Am. The mountain at the center of their land, which was the source of warmth, air, and water, was called the *har*. The bison were called *para* and the sheep *keepsa*."

"It appeared that the Am had no writing or money or technical culture whatever (if you except one woman's effort to make wings out of banana leaves). All their needs were provided for by the natural life around them. Their main communal activity seemed to be choral singing. I can't describe that glorious sound, but Yaffa translated one of the anthems they sang facing the har as,

O mountain, fount of all things good,
Preserve our local neighborhood."

"Nights on the moon are also 14 times as long as Earth nights," Morey continues. "The Am sleep suspended upside-down from tree branches. Yaffa found it hilarious that I could never quite get the hang of it, so to speak. I chose to sleep instead on the front seat of the Albino."

"During the long night, the Am would wake at times to forage for fruit, sing, and make love by the glow of the har, that of the stars and sometimes a faint blue emanation from the Earth, which was only occasionally visible through the canopy of clouds. They called the Earth *olom*, knew nothing about it, and despite my efforts to tell them, didn't want to know."

"Before long, I had settled into the languorous rhythm of life on the moon. My curiosity had rewarded me beyond all expectation. This demi-paradise on the moon flooded me with a wealth of new direct sensory experience that would have made John Locke proud of me. The weather was balmy, the food was delicious, and Yaffa and I were in love."

"Yet curiosity still tugged at me. What would I find on Mars or Venus, Jupiter or Saturn? They could wait, I thought. Life here with Yaffa was perfection. Then one day I noticed that the Albino was no longer where I had left it. It had disappeared. That settles it, I thought, I shall stay here forever. Could it be, I wondered, that a machine powered by nothingness might spontaneously turn into nothing itself?"

"Then I saw the Albino high overhead. It slowly settled into its former place by the brook. Two moonyouths emerged from it laughing merrily."

"I commended the boys for their unusual curiosity and gently upbraided them for taking the Albino without my permission. They feigned incomprehension, or perhaps truly didn't understand me, since the Am had no word for theft. I removed the Albino's starting key and put it in my trouser pocket."

"Where the boys had been they wouldn't or couldn't say beyond 'up.' But somewhere they had found a strange object: a box with a window on one side through which one could see only darkness. They called it 'the looking at thing.'"

"As you can imagine, their finding that box raised many questions, but the boys wouldn't let me touch their treasure. Instead they set it down in a tree and spent a long time gazing at 'the looking at thing,' which appeared to be completely inert."

"They struck it with their hands, but it made a dull, unsatisfying noise. Then they began laughing again and flew with it up into the air and dropped it into the lake."

"The long lunar days and nights continued on in serene uneventfulness, until one morning Yaffa announced to me that she was pregnant. I confess I felt a small surge of pride to think that I would be the first human ever to sire a hostage to fortune on another world."

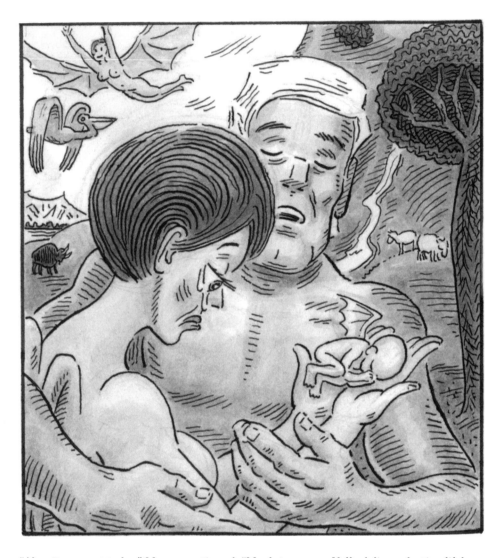

"Alas, it was not to be," Morey continued. "Much too soon, Yaffa delivered a tiny lifeless creature that had only one wing. Yaffa wept bitterly and I did what little I could to console her."

"As was the custom of the Am, she flew to the top of the har and dropped our dead baby into its luminous cone."

"Soon, Yaffa had regained her former cheerful demeanor and was happily flitting about with the other Am in their extraordinary aerial acrobatics."

"The Am had a game involving juggling fruit while they were in flight. Yaffa was brilliantly adept at it, and I became a kind of connoisseur of their lunar sports. Then one day something terrible happened."

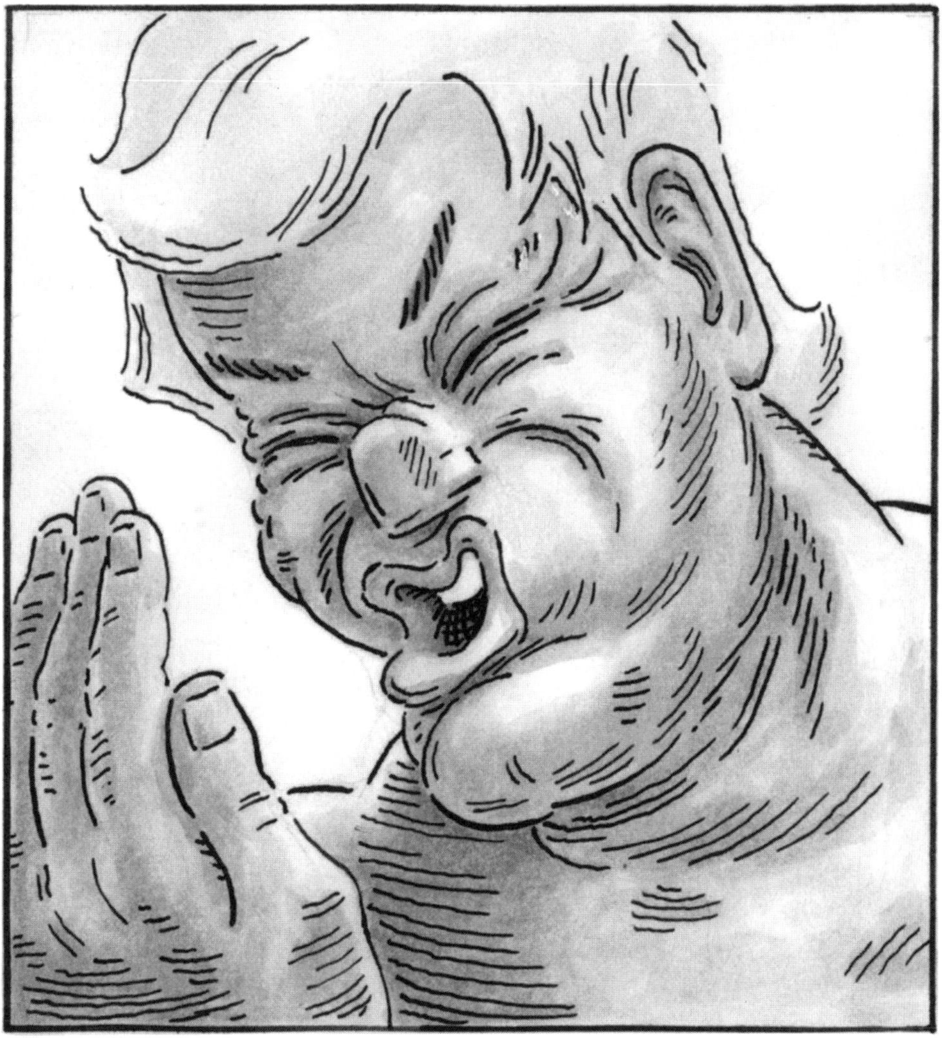

“I sneezed.”

"Yaffa drew back in fear. It was a noise she had never heard before. I excused myself and laughed. I told her she must say 'gesundheit' and she said, 'Gesundheit' in her lilting lunar accent."

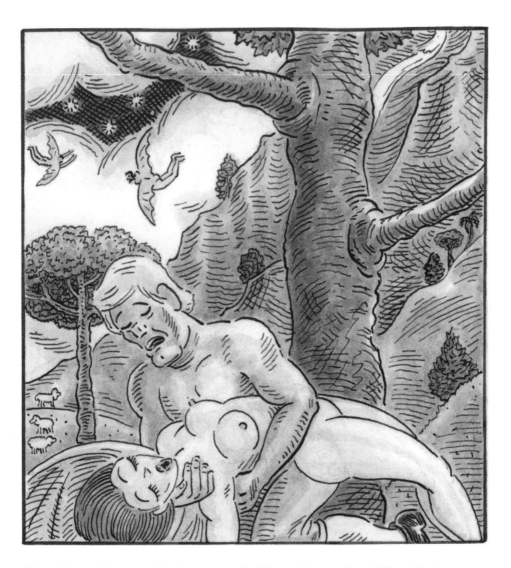

"Then she said she wasn't feeling very well. Although it was the middle of the day, she took to her tree saying she needed to rest, and hung there swinging quietly. Then she fell to the ground, whispered weakly to me, 'Sam, Sam, Sam,' and in moments was stone-cold dead."

"I was stunned with grief. What had happened? I gently placed Yaffa on the front seat of the Albino, started the engine, slowly flew to the top of the har and, tears streaming from my eyes, pushed her beautiful, lifeless body into its glowing cone."

"When I returned the vehicule to its spot by the brook, I saw all around me Am staggering and falling on their faces or on their winged backs. They were all dying. Had my one sneeze released a contagion into their world which they were powerless to resist? Or could it have been the ham?"

"Those Am still able-bodied enough formed airborne processions carrying the dead to the har and dropping them in. Some, with their last measure of strength, threw themselves in as well."

"It was a scene of unimaginable horror. All the animals started to die. Birds dropped out of the air. Dead fish floated on the surface of the lake. The trees instantly wilted and fell over. I, Samuel Morey, a human being from New Hampshire, was an absolute plague on the moon."

"Overburdened with the dead, the mountain began to fulminate and then slowly collapse. I rushed to the Albino and rose to a height where I could watch in safety as a spreading tide of molten lava caused the lake to boil over."

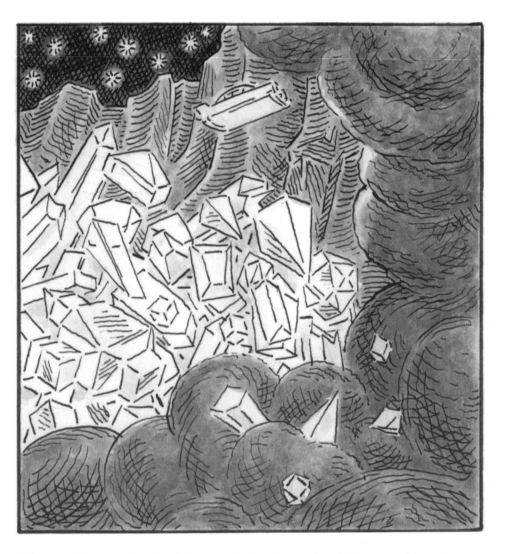

"The sparkling crystal walls of the great basin fell inward and disappeared into the immense cloud of steam, smoke and dust that filled it."

"After the dust settled and the steam and smoke dissipated, all I could see beneath me was a barren gray crater indistinguishable from the thousands, even millions of others that pitted the surface of the moon."

"Yaffa, the Am, the amazing lunar flora and fauna were all dead. I killed them. I cursed the goddamned curiosity that led me to bring about this calamity. I cursed John Locke whose writings had encouraged me to directly experience things that I would have been better off merely dreaming about, or imagining, or perhaps just reading about in a book. I cursed my terrible, destructive, misguided self. I pointed the Albino toward Earth and headed home."

"What a sad, awful story," says Charity Moore after a long silence. "You wrote it," says Locke, "You wrote the story in the *Edinburgh Journal of Science*." "I not only wrote it, I printed it," says Samuel Morey gesturing toward some type cases and a small printing press in a dark corner of the house. "You might say it was a limited edition."

"But, in heaven's name, why?" Locke asks. "Simply to be believed and then not believed," says Morey. "Pride demanded that I tell the world what I saw on the moon. Shame forbade me from admitting to having destroyed it all. Herschel's sojourn in Africa offered the chance for me to frame the tale with all that ridiculous business about the telescope."

"You see," says Morey, "there is a certain hierarchy of truth. At the bottom is the false story that is not believed. That is the absurd realm of fairy tales and fiction. Then there is a case of false things that are believed to be true: the province of religion and superstition and common lies. The everyday world of true things that are believed to be true is almost too trivial to mention. But at the highest level exist true things that will never be believed—things that are unknown or unknowable or simply, as we say, 'incredible.' My tale of the inhabitants of the moon is in that category."

"But why was it necessary to turn me into the world's biggest liar?" Locke asks. "Well," says Morey, "it was too late to punish John Locke for being a dangerous fool, so his great-great-grandson would have to be ruined instead." "Thank you very much," says Richard Locke.

"Having once believed in the moon story, Mr. Locke, you clearly do not now, do you, despite all my excellent detail and elaboration?" says Morey. "Of course not," says Locke, "There isn't a bit of proof." "That's where you are wrong," says Morey.

Morey turns away and calls out, "Angus!" From the dark recesses of the house emerges the figure of a man dressed in full Scottish regalia. "A Scotsman—The Scotsman," Locke exclaims. "Yes," says Morey, after introducing Locke and Charity to the man. "You might say that Angus is my personal assistant."

"It was Angus who gave the *Journal* to the newsboy. He followed you to Monsieur Audubon's house. That Frenchman is quite an artist, by the way. Angus spied on Audubon, and at an opportune moment bought the great blue heron and brought it here." "Well, what does that prove?" Locke asks.

"When I told you about my return from the moon, I left out a detail," says Morey. "As I fled the catastrophe that I had created, I looked over my shoulder at the receding disc of the moon for the first time and saw, huddled in a corner of the back seat of the Albino, a small Am child trembling with fear—apparently, the one moon creature impervious to the plague had taken shelter with, of all people, me."

"Angus, would you be good enough to remove your Inverness?" Angus drops his cape, revealing two leathery bat wings folded against his back. "My God," says Charity, "He's one of the moonpeople!" "Aye, 'tis true, lassie," says Angus stripping off the rest of his clothing. "I taught him to speak with a brogue to complete the Highlander masquerade," says Morey.

"Sadly, to cover my tracks, it was necessary to eliminate some witnesses. The typographer who copied the *Journal* had to go. Likewise, the newsboy who saw Angus, and the foul constable who was asking too many questions. I wouldn't call it murder—it was simply a matter of Angus lifting them to a certain height and then letting them go. With so many deaths of innocents already on my conscience, a few more didn't matter to me." "You crazy bastard," says Locke.

"And now," says Morey, "you will please hand over that *Edinburgh Journal of Science*, Mr. Locke."

"Never!" says Charity, pulling a pistol from her bag, and training it on Morey. Locke is as astonished by this as are Morey and Angus.

With a swift move, Angus knocks the gun out of Charity's hand.

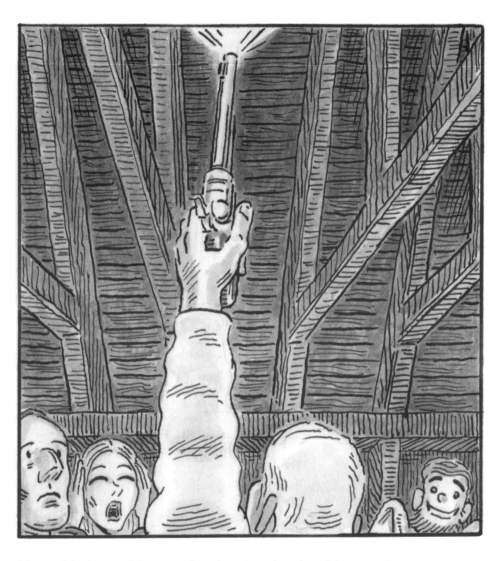

Morey picks it up and fires two shots into the rafters in quick succession.

Morey examines the gun. "Very clever indeed," he says. "It's called a 'revolver,'" says Charity. "I bought it from a Mr. Colt who has a shop in Hartford."

"The *Journal,* please, Mr. Locke," Morey says. Locke gives it to him.

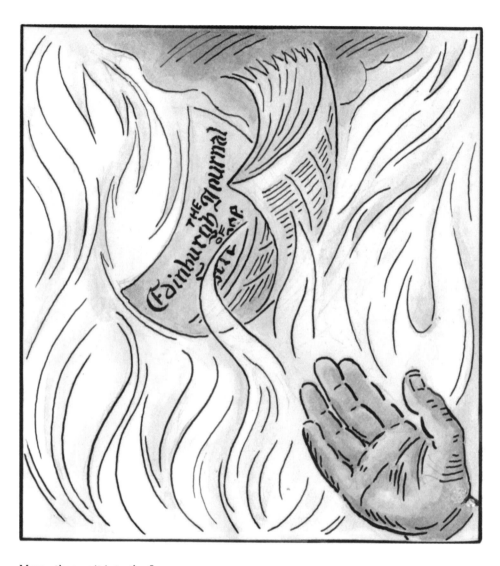

Morey throws it into the fire.

Night has fallen. Morey orders Locke and Charity to put on their warm clothing. Then, carrying a lantern, he shows them out of the house at gunpoint. Angus follows.

They trudge through the snow to one of Morey's sheds and he opens its doors.

Inside is a sleek white machine, something like the autovehicule that fell through the ice, but bigger, with vertical fish-like fins at the rear and no wheels whatsoever. It is the Albino.

"Get in," says Morey, waving the 'revolver.' Locke and Charity get into the back seat, Morey sits behind the ship's wheel-like device and Angus, holding the gun, sits next to Morey. Morey inserts a key into a keyhole and the machine begins to vibrate silently. Then it starts to rise off the ground a little and slowly moves out of the shed.

A full moon is rising over the hills. The Albino tilts upward until it is aimed directly at the moon. Then it starts to pick up speed.

The Albino goes faster and faster. Locke and Charity, Morey and Angus are pressed forcefully back into their seats. The acceleration continues and then levels off. Now the passengers feel themselves floating out of their seats. Locke looks at an indicator in front of Morey that says they are traveling at 100,000 miles an hour. He comments on it and Morey says. "And we're only in first gear."

Soon they are approaching the disc of the moon, which has grown to fill the entire front window of the Albino.

The machine slows down and takes a curving path that carries them around the orb's back side—always a mystery to mankind—but, seen now only by starlight, is much like the familiar side.

Emerging into the light, the Albino slows down further. The surface of the moon is truly dismal gray and dappled with craters of every size. "There is the Mare Imbrium," says Morey, indicating a somewhat dark area, and then, spiraling downward, he begins to circle one particular crater that is much like the others. "And that was once the land of the Am," says Morey. His face pressed to the window, Angus begins to silently weep.

The Albino travels slower and lower until they are nearly grazing the surface of the crater, but there is in fact no sign that anything has ever existed there but rocks and rubble—no part of a luminous mountain, no remnant of a river or a lake, no fragment of a giant crystal—nothing.

Then Charity sees something and points downward.

With the Albino hovering only inches above a peak bordering the reputed crater of the Am, its passengers clearly see the remains of a cat—Morey's long lost tabby.

Morey abruptly tilts the Albino upward and soon it is hurtling at great speed toward the Earth whose disc is four times larger in the sky than the moon ever appears from Earth.

The machine slows to a moderate speed as it penetrates the Earth's atmosphere and, as the Albino continues to descend, the Earth assumes a map-like aspect. Through the clouds, the passengers can distinguish the outline of the east coast of North America, and soon Locke can see they are following the path of the Connecticut River down its fertile valley. It is morning.

Morey slows further and then hovers just above his Orford farmstead before rising again and heading southward.

380

The Albino continues down the Connecticut until they cross Long Island Sound.
Then Morey turns it abruptly westward and they follow Long Island until they reach
the estuary of the Hudson River. "New York City," says Locke, looking down at it and
breaking the silence that has pervaded the Albino since it left the moon.

As they fly low over New Jersey, Morey speaks. "Quite a journey, my friends, wouldn't you agree?" he says. "But I am sorry to say we are now approaching its sad, inevitable conclusion."

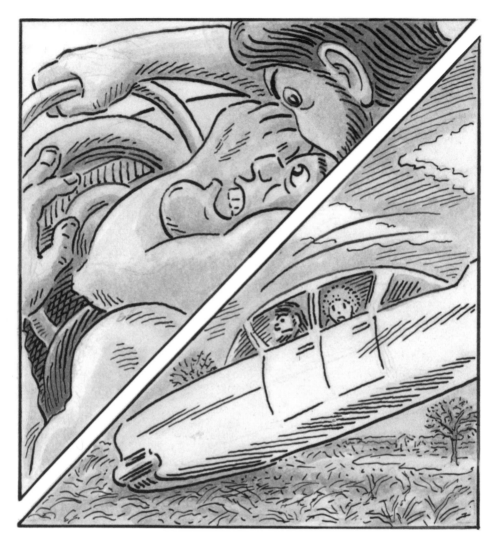

All at once, Angus puts Morey into a headlock, takes control of the Albino and brings it down with a thump in a field of corn stubble.

Throwing open a rear door, he shouts, "Run!" at Locke and Charity, and they do.

Regaining control of his machine and now holding Angus at gunpoint, Morey puts the Albino into a steep climb and then levels off.

They cross Delaware Bay and then Chesapeake Bay to the District of Columbia where, far below, they can see the distinctive green dome of the Capitol.

Then Morey puts the Albino into a screaming dive. A terrified Angus jumps out of the machine at the next to last moment.

Morey plunges the Albino into a large brick building, destroying it, his machine, and himself in a fiery explosion. The building was Blodgett's Hotel, better known as the United States Patent Office.

Over the next few days, Locke and Charity gradually make their way back to New York. As they walk up the front path to Chelsea, Charity says to Locke, "Perhaps you had better wait outside for a moment."

Opening the front door, the butler gasps at the sight of her. "Miss Charity!" he exclaims. Clement Moore comes to the door, and in a transport of joy throws his arms around his daughter.

He had been in deep mourning, convinced that Charity had perished in the great New York fire. His friend Da Ponte has also recently died. Charity tells her father that, after the fire, she had been knocked unconscious by a falling timber, had lost her memory, and only this day regained it. She is delighted to be home. They embrace again. "There is someone else who would like to see you," she says.

"Keep away from me, you monster of evil!" says Moore as Richard Locke walks in. "Sir, I would like to ask you for your daughter's hand in marriage," says Locke. "Are you out of your mind?" says Moore. "Never, ever, even over my dead body," says Moore. "Sir, may I have a private word with you?" says Locke.

Locke takes Moore to one side and says a few words softly into his ear.

"Well, well, my boy, you are a welcome addition to my family," says Moore, "No need to stand on ceremony—you and Charity shall be married immediately."

With the butler and Sara Fortune serving as witnesses, the Reverend Moore marries the couple on the spot. Locke and Charity kiss.

Later, as they stroll the grounds of Chelsea, Charity asks Locke, "Whatever did you say to father to bring about such an abrupt change of heart?" "You will never know," says Locke. (What he said was, "I can prove that *The Night Before Christmas* was written by Major Henry Livingston.") Then Charity tells Locke her secret: she is pregnant. "If the child is a boy, let's not call him Herschel," says Locke. It was and they didn't.

EPILOGUE

Jean Jacques Audubon continued traveling west without success in his search for a specimen of the California condor. Then one day, in the Mojave desert, he was sure he had spotted one overhead. He took careful aim with his rifle and fired.

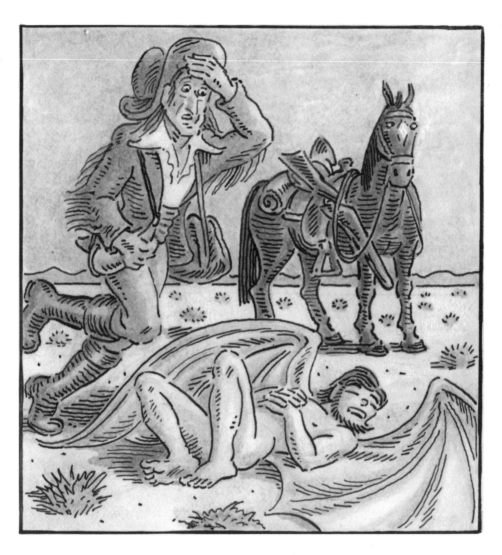

Approaching his dead prey, he was horrified to see he had killed a naked human being with the leathery wings of a bat. Where had he seen such a thing before, he thought, and then he remembered that he had once drawn things like it from a printed description. And the creature's face somehow reminded him of a Scotsman he once met. Resolving never to speak of the incident, Audubon buried Angus and went on looking for the elusive condor.

THE
WHOLE
TRUTH

The "Great Moon Hoax" of 1835 was the most successful newspaper hoax in history. It permanently raised the circulation of *The New York Sun* (which surely was its purpose) and was widely believed as it traveled around the world for years. At the time, many of the signal achievements of the 19th century still lay well in the future. Railroads were in their infancy. The telegraph, photography, the findings of Darwin and Pasteur all came later. Andrew Jackson was President. The steamboat was the summit of technology. News traveled slowly. When John Herschel (the Einstein of his time) finally learned of the moon story in South Africa, he good-naturedly remarked, "It is too bad my real discoveries here won't be that exciting." Later in life he complained that, no matter where he went, people wanted to ask him only about the bat-people on the moon.

Richard Locke was certainly the author of the hoax, although, depending on whom you believe, he never admitted to it, or did so only once when he was drunk. In my story he didn't write it. Locke was married and the father of a daughter at the time. In my story he is single. *The Sun* never retracted the moon story.

Phineas Barnum was showing Joice Heth, his first "curiosity," at Niblo's Garden at this time. Whether Joice was George Washington's nurse is questionable to say the least. Charity's indignant letter to the editor is taken verbatim from a real letter written by another person and published in *The Sun*.

The Sun's original series was unillustrated, although it referred to illustrations in the *Edinburgh Journal of Science*, a scholarly journal that had actually ceased publication in 1833. A subsequent pamphlet version of the story (it sold 60,000 copies) did contain a few crude, uncredited illustrations probably done by an artist in the print shop of Nathaniel Currier (Mr. Currier met Mr. Ives later on). Currier was known to be a friend of *The Sun*'s publisher Benjamin Day (whose son of the same name later invented the benday printing process).

Clement Moore did have a daughter named Charity, but she died in childhood. Benjamin Moore, the housepaint man, was Clement's grandson, rather than his son as I have it.

Timothy Fortune was an African American typographer and journalist of the latter half of the 19th century. Fortune the typesetter in my story is his hypothetical father. I've imagined Billy Tweed, the newsboy, as an early version of the man who later dominated New York City, the notorious "Boss" Tweed.

The Yale scientists Loomis, Olmsted and Silliman were all real people as was Constable Jacob Hays. Samuel Colt did introduce the first revolver in Hartford in 1835.

Richard Locke did write a hoax about Mungo Park (a real person) that attracted no attention. Since I was unable to find it, my version is, I confess, a fake hoax.

The total eclipse of the sun I describe was actually seen in New York in 1834.

Jean Jacques Audubon was in and out of New York during this period. He was, in fact, rumored to be the missing dauphin of France (he wasn't) and to have studied with Ingres (he didn't)—claims he never denied.

I have streamlined *The Sun*'s account of Herschel's supposed discoveries on the moon to make it slightly more plausible to modern readers. However, all the elements I present are from the original, and everything in quotes is verbatim from *The Sun*'s story.

Clement Moore was in fact the patron of Lorenzo Da Ponte, the Mozart librettist who taught Italian at Columbia for many years. While Da Ponte did live in England for a time, he was not there when Mozart was, and Da Ponte's encounter with William Herschel is entirely fictional. Da Ponte was once in fact in the distillery business in Pennsylvania, and his tale of Casanova swindling an old woman is taken from Da Ponte's memoirs.

While a religious group in Connecticut did in fact make plans at the time to communicate with the moon-dwellers, Moore, to the best of my knowledge, had no part in it. He was, however, the author of *The Compendious Lexicon of the Hebrew Language*. In Donald Foster's book "Author Unknown," Foster makes a compelling case for *The Night Before Christmas* having been written by Major Henry Livingston. The image of the mansion at Chelsea is based on a sketch by one of Moore's daughters.

Pierre Toussaint, the Haitian hairdresser, was a real person, although his interest in abolition and Toussaint L'Ouverture is entirely conjectural. Pierre's remains are currently in the Vatican while he is being considered for sainthood.

Julia Ward, an early abolitionist, did live in New York at this time. She later married Samuel Gridley Howe (who turned out to be a cad). Julia subsequently wrote "The Battle Hymn of the Republic."

The image of the exterior of the Bowery Theatre is based on a contemporary drawing. The image of its interior is based on a painting of the Park Theater from the same period. The Bowery did put on a show called *Lunar Discoveries* at the time, but its actual content is lost to history.

Edgar Allan Poe was in New York during this period. His young cousin, Virginia Clemm, became his wife. In a remarkable essay titled *Eureka*, Poe eerily foretold the findings of 20th century physics and cosmology. Poe also wrote a profile of Locke and an account of the moon hoax that were both published about nine years after the events in my story.

The canal on Canal Street was probably filled in by 1835. The Castle Garden (Castle Clinton) was not roofed over as I show it until sometime after 1835. The Moon Pie was probably not invented until the 20th century but I could not resist including it.

Charles Goodyear did have a shop in New York where he eventually developed the vulcanization process.

Much of lower Manhattan was, in fact, destroyed in the Great Fire of December 1835.

Samuel Morey was a New Hampshire inventor who built a working steamboat before Robert Fulton, which the world chose to ignore. He also prematurely invented and patented the internal combustion engine, which, likewise, attracted no interest. The United States Patent Office did mysteriously burn to the ground in 1836 taking all its secrets with it.

Dan Sickles was, in fact, a student of Lorenzo Da Ponte. He became a Civil War general and lost a leg at Gettysburg. He married Da Ponte's granddaughter, Theresa Bagioli, who later had an affair with Phillip Barton Key. Sickles killed Key and was subsequently acquitted of murder on the basis of temporary insanity. But that is another story.

—R.G., *November 2013*

ROBERT GROSSMAN

Robert Grossman (1940 – 2018) was a renowned award-winning artist whose career spanned over fifty years. He grew up in Brooklyn, NY, attended Yale University, and went on to illustrate over 500 magazine covers. His work was distinguished by its humor and strong graphic style. Publications that featured his distinctive, whimsical, and satirical caricatures, cartoons, illustrations, and sculptures include *The New York Times, The New Yorker, Rolling Stone, Sports Illustrated, The Nation, Time, Newsweek, Esquire, Playboy, The Atlantic, National Lampoon, The New York Observer, Forbes, Natural History,* and many others. He was also a contributing editor for *New York* magazine for many years. His work has appeared in books, advertising, on greeting cards, board games, record albums and movie posters, including the classic cover for The Firesign Theatre's comedy record *Don't Crush That Dwarf, Hand Me the Pliers* and the iconic poster for the film *AIRPLANE!*

Grossman's children's book *What Can a Hippopotamus Be?* (Simon and Schuster) has received international acclaim and his distinctive illustrations have appeared in numerous anthologies, beginning with *The Beatles Illustrated Lyrics* in 1969. Grossman often worked as an animator as well: his film *Jimmy the C* received an Academy Award nomination in 1978, and his company Grossman Brothers produced a string of memorable TV commercials in the 1980s. His work has been widely exhibited, with a solo show at Galerie Vontobel in Zurich, Switzerland, in 1980 and recognition by the Smithsonian Institution. Most recently, his work was on display at the Walt Disney Family Museum in San Francisco. He has inspired many of the top illustrators working today, and was a major influence for Terry Gilliam's Monty Python art. He was one of six inductees to the Airbrush Hall of Fame in 1999, and an endowment in his name, The Robert Grossman Award for Satire, is awarded annually for the best work of satire done by a Yale undergraduate. His work can be enjoyed online at www.robertgrossman.com.

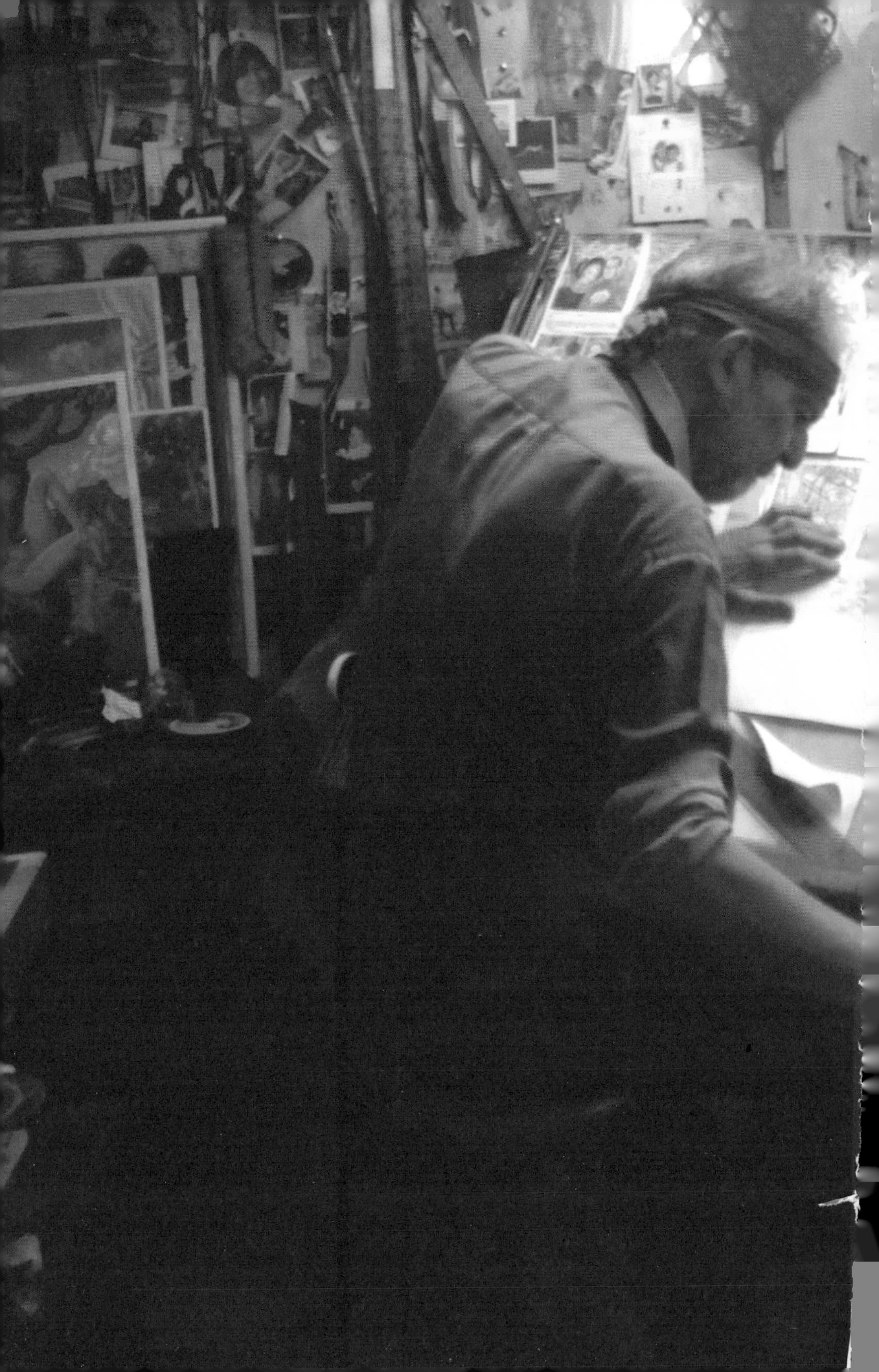